VOICES OF (

The Story of the Fifteenth Street School

Rachel and Wilbur Rippy

To children everywhere

"I do not mean to offer a model of what is needed
and is good for a school,
but simply to furnish an actual description of the school.
I presume that such descriptions may have their use."

– Leo Tolstoy,
on his school at Yasnaya Polyana

Contents

2 The School in Action   63

3 The Arts: A Child's First Language   103

Acknowledgments

This book has been enriched by the thoughts and efforts of many people who worked to make it come alive.

Peter Lavery's trenchant analyses and ideas helped me transform Wilbur's notes and my early drafts into a readable book. Maureen Brady further assisted with her perceptive edits.

My Bank Street College colleagues Stacy Miller, Ann Marie Mott and Katherine O'Donnell and my writing colleagues, Ana Diz, Carolyn Capstick Meehan, Reginetta Haboucha, Gail Miller, Susan Weiman and John Williams gave their time and support, sensitively reading drafts, offering wise comments and astute insights.

Paul Fusco generously gave permission for the use of his photographs in this book, and Anthony Fusco and Marina (Fusco) Nims helped with resolving technical issues.

Allan Converse, Celia Converse, Robert Dewey, Michael Krieg and Bill Schenker, graduates of the Fifteenth Street School, described their thoughts and recollections about the school, helping the book to resonate with their experiences.

Drawing on their extensive research into children's natural ways of learning, Peter Gray and Alexander Khost contributed their thoughts to this book. Peter Gray wrote about the relevance of the Fifteenth Street School to current day education and Alexander Khost about the practice of self-directed education in past and present settings. David Wolf generously gave wise counsel and legal advice.

Ruth Adler, Erica Alliston, Juliana Alexander, Joe Baez, Laura Bigras, David Colbert, Sheila Epstein, Carolyn Fleischman, Meg Gillette, Elizabeth Green, Cristina Gupta, Amanda Hammett, Mimi Miller, Geraldine Light, Margaret Lundin, Ed Rogers, Sandra Sanford and William Schurtman offered interest and encouragement that sustained me through the long process of writing this book.

Michael Krieg stood by steadfastly with ideas and helped me sustain faith in the project. My lifelong friend Zohra Lampert provided continuous emotional and intellectual support and improved my manuscript with her deep understanding of life and its complexities.

Cynthia Graae, with her spirit of enthusiasm, and writer's grasp of the creation of literature extended her friendship and unstinting assistance. Rachel Theilheimer offered unwavering support many long years and gave me the courage to complete the writing of this story. Her generative insights enabled me to expand and deepen the scope and conception of this book.

Jonathan Beard contributed his expert copy editing. Thanks to Meryl Pollen for her helpful advice.

Finally, David Tabatsky took the reins and ably guided the process of turning a manuscript into a book.

I am grateful to all of you and the many others, too numerous to name, who made this possible.

Foreword

More than fifty years ago, children told and wrote stories, designed their own science experiences, collaborated with one another and their teachers, and made all kinds of discoveries at the Fifteenth Street School. Best of all, their days were filled with humor, warmth and creative thinking. Rachel and Wilbur Rippy, the authors of *Voices of Children: The Story of the Fifteenth Street School*, who participated in founding the school, invite readers in to see adults and children working and learning side by side. These teachers, dedicated to supporting children's self-directed learning, have written a book about the past that has relevance for today's programs for children. In it, they offer a vivid description of the voices and actions that once filled the school and that seem as alive now as they were then.

Using stories, photos, and samples of children's work, the Rippys convey their views of children and how to teach them. Over the course of a decade, at the Fifteenth Street School and elsewhere before that, their collaborative work with children gave them opportunities to observe children's ability to direct their own learning.

The book illustrates self-directed learning; that is, when children pursue the knowledge that they want in ways the children construct for themselves—with supportive adults providing materials, comments, and questions. The Rippys demonstrate how this approach and their work with children draw from the thinking of educators and philosophers such as Jean Jacques Rousseau, John Dewey, and A.S. Neill, and present-day researchers such as Alison Gopnik and Peter Gray.

Rachel Rippy narrates the story of the inception and growth of the school. She interweaves her late husband Wilbur's observations and reflections with her own descriptions, recollections and elaborations. Rachel animates the space and the people in it as she describes children's self-directed activities. She illuminates the thinking and rethinking behind the spaces, materials, and interactions that made children's autonomy possible. The children's voices that ring true throughout the book, in combination with those of the Rippys, recall a hopeful era when thoughtful educational experimentation was possible. At the same time, they offer inspiration to current and future teachers who can imagine applications to their own work.

Voices of Children is a collaboration in the spirit of the school that is at the heart of this story. Together, Wilbur's observations and Rachel's narration tell the school's story, and several present-day voices of now-adult Fifteenth Street School students show how much such a school can continue to mean to the recipients of that form of education. Revealing children's perspectives along with those of the adults who learned alongside them, this book demonstrates how teachers can enable children's inherent curiosity and love of learning to flourish when they trust children to take charge of their learning.

Rachel Theilheimer
Professor Emerita, Borough of Manhattan Community College,
City University of New York

Teaching and learning are not the opposite of each other.
They are so intertwined.
When I teach, I always learn something new.
I find myself saying things to my students that I didn't know I knew.
And maybe I didn't or maybe I just know for the first time . . .
when I teach, I learn, when I learn, I teach.

– Leonard Bernstein

Chapter 1

Origins and Inspiration

In September 1964, the first *Summerhill* inspired school in New York City opened its doors to twenty-eight boys and girls, aged four to six. Everyone was excited and apprehensive as the staff welcomed the families to the four-story building we had turned into a school.

With my husband Wilbur and me, they explored the freshly painted rooms facing the street and leafy backyards of New York City's Chelsea area and examined the blocks, puzzles, and math and reading materials we had assembled. We relaxed, as all seemed to fall into place, and we talked and laughed getting acquainted. After a while, the parents left, confident that their children would be cared for. By three p.m., going home time, most everyone looked forward to returning the next day.

During our next four years at the school, Wilbur collected the children's stories and artworks and recorded his observations and comments about the events that unfolded there. When he died in 2006, he left drafts for a book he hoped to publish, and, continuing our long-standing collaboration, I undertook to complete the task as the co-narrator of our story.

According to Wilbur, "Children are creatures of movement and activity, of observation, of inquiry, of social connection, who seek the skill, understanding and competency needed in the social world they inhabit. The free school is brought into being by adults *and* children. The Fifteenth Street School will be a place where children find resources to create the images of their world and develop their creative, literary and thinking skills through the arts and their use of pretend, from its earliest forms of house-play to staged dramatic presentations."

I have wondered if this small, privately funded, independent school with a privileged student body has any relevance to our time.

Does anything that occurred there apply to our competitive world of high stakes testing or to the many children around the world forced into servitude and hard labor?

In a free society, schools such as this serve as laboratories for new ideas. And presently, researchers in early brain development corroborate the idea that play, open-ended inquiry, and social interaction are crucial in developing the neural structures children need to absorb and process information and engage in critical thinking. The children's expressions of goodwill at the Fifteenth Street School in the 1960s, and their quest to discover and create, represent universal experiences and values. Thus, as those children's voices come vividly to life again in the following pages, they are as relevant and important today as they were five decades ago.

Beginnings

The Fifteenth Street School originated when the actor and TV host Orson Bean began looking for a suitable school for his five-year-old daughter. While researching the field, he found the book *Summerhill* by the Scottish author and educator A.S. Neill, published in the U.S. in 1960. Neill's story about his school and how he arrived at his philosophy of non-compulsory education sparked Orson's thinking.

Neill began his teaching in conventional schools and worked with delinquent teens for many years. His experience with children and research in the field led him to believe that children develop best when they are free to direct their own lives and learning. In 1926, he founded his boarding school Summerhill in Suffolk, England, and put his ideas into practice. At Summerhill, children would be able to govern themselves and their learning. "It is the idea of non-interference with the growth of the child and non-pressure on the child that has made the school what it is," Neill wrote. Influenced by Neill's example, Orson resolved to create a setting in the city where young children could grow and learn at their own pace. He began by seeking experienced teachers to shape this idea into a reality.

Voices of Children

When Wilbur and I had read Neill's writings: *A Dominie's Log* (1916), *The Problem Teacher* (1939), and *Summerhill,* his empathic connection with and understanding of children resonated with our own thoughts. In our years of teaching, we had observed children taking initiative in their learning: spontaneously experimenting with words and materials; inventing and organizing their own games, dramas, stories, and art projects; and co-operating to resolve complex problems. These observations and Neill's ideas about self-direction inspired our vision of a school where children had the time, space. and support to explore and expand on their ideas.

Wilbur and I met through the Teacher Education Program at Bank Street College in 1953. After we completed our studies, we worked with pre-school and elementary-age children as teachers and administrators in public and private schools. When we heard of Orson's plans, we were intrigued with the possibilities and arranged to meet him. We discussed our ideas and found that we all had a similar vision for the direction the school should follow, and Orson asked us to join him in his enterprise. At last, after a decade of teaching, the school we had imagined was about to become a reality. What follows is the story of the path that brought us there.

Rachel And Wilbur: Developing Our Thinking

Wilbur and I grew up in different settings, he in the American South and I in Europe and then New York City. Though we both attended similar conventional schools, our life experiences and readings led us into new ways of viewing the world and becoming interested in the process of learning.

Wilbur was born in 1923 and grew up in Nashville, Tennessee, during the difficult days of the Depression. He attended conventional schools that used the rote system of instruction, and he was not motivated to learn in this pedagogical setting. He sought out his own reading materials from the popular literature of the day and attended band concerts where he heard local bluegrass and jazz. When Wilbur received a trumpet on his thirteenth birthday, he learned to play all styles of music and practiced to perform in local dance bands. He hoped to study music in college, but when Pearl Harbor was attacked in 1941, he changed his plans and enlisted in the Navy as a bandsman.

At the Bremerton Naval Base, Wilbur learned damage-control skills needed on a warship and played in the band. While on leave in nearby Seattle, he visited a library where he met Miss Mayo, a librarian who offered to help him find books that interested him. She introduced him to the novel *You Can't Go Home Again* by Thomas Wolfe, a fellow Southerner. It was Wilbur's first encounter with this style of fiction and he wanted more. Miss Mayo followed up with works of Hemingway and Steinbeck, great American authors who spoke to him of new worlds and insights into the human condition.

As part of the war effort, libraries reached out to assist servicemen, and when Wilbur was assigned to the battleship USS *Maryland*, Miss Mayo continued her work by sending him books through the mail. Sometimes the books were delivered to the ship, and sometimes they were waiting when the ship docked stateside or in Hawaii for refueling or repairs.

During the next eighteen months of active duty, as the battleship cruised the deadly waters of the Pacific War theater, Wilbur found time to read novels that stirred his imagination while calming his anxiety.

He wrote about his life on the ship:

◄ Waiting is the story of our lives. Waiting for the war to end. Waiting to return to the States. Waiting for liberty, for leave, for transfer. Waiting to be shredded, blown to pieces, smoked out, suffocated. Breathing ceases. Heart pounds. We wait. ►

At last, after more than three years at war, Wilbur was discharged. The lively teenager had morphed into a somber young man shaken by the violence he had experienced and questioning the nature of existence. He sought a new direction in his life and found inspiration in his love of literature, which had sustained him through hard times. Backed by benefits from the GI Bill, he enrolled at The New School for Social Research in New York City to study English Literature.

It was 1946, and Wilbur flourished in the New York City atmosphere, with its innovative music and art scene. When he graduated from the New School and thought about the future, he decided he wanted to live in New York. While he was trying to figure out how he might earn a livelihood, an Early Childhood teacher he knew suggested he visit the Harriet Johnson Nursery School, an affiliate of Bank Street. There he noticed a four-year-old boy sawing wood.

Wilbur describes his experience:

◄ He was sawing away, so serious and intent that I asked him the novice's question, "What are you making?" He paused and pointed to the floor. "Sawdust," he said. It was so. Later, he pinched up the sawdust and placed it in the cellophane wrapper I removed from my cigarette pack.

Though he could not tell me that he enjoyed the rhythmic push of the saw through the wood, his sense of mastery and the transformation of something into something else, his child mind reasoned that making sawdust was a logical result of sawing wood. Memories flashed: my father teaching me to saw, scrounging wood with my friends to make scooters, go-carts, and toy rafts.

I saw there was something going on in education I had not remotely been aware of. It stunned me. I realized that it was the opposite of what it was like when I went to school. Could school be a place where children wanted to learn? ►

Until that time, Wilbur had thought of schools as places designed to fill "empty vessels." Now he watched the teacher as she listened to the children's thoughts and helped them to follow their interests. He realized that, like the wise Miss Mayo, teachers could be mentors who inspired children to expand their worlds.

Soon, he enrolled at Bank Street College where he learned about the theory of Progressive Education based on the concept that children learn through interactive experiences. By 1953, Wilbur was teaching the six-to eight-year-old group at the Boardman School, an independent school on Manhattan's Upper East Side.

At the same time, I received a BA from the University of Chicago where I studied literature and philosophy in the Great Books Program. I was interested in writing but was at sea about what to do next. I found the answer when I traveled to Israel and met a teacher who told me about Bank Street and Neill's writings.

Like Wilbur, I was not happy with my time in the conventional schools I attended, first in Antwerp, Belgium, and from sixth grade on in New York City. My ideas about schooling were jolted when I read about Neill's work with children, and I thought that teaching could be creative, challenging work. It wasn't long until I applied and was accepted at Bank Street.

I had a rather rocky start in my student teaching, as the classrooms and teachers I was assigned to did not match my idealized vision of life in school. My advisor, Mrs. Winsor, was concerned because I was not developing the skills I needed for teaching, and I will always be grateful to her for persevering and divining that Wilbur would be a teacher from whom I could learn.

My spirit lifted immediately when I entered Wilbur's classroom with its sound of children humming as they worked. Some were sawing and hammering, some painting, some block building, and others, reading. In the center of the room, was an assemblage of tables converted to a ship that was part of the class study of transportation. On deck were handwritten signs and a compass and nets, and some of the children were climbing down ladders to "repair" the lower deck under the table. Much of the skills instruction in reading, writing, and math was connected to research about this project. Using a central topic to integrate the curriculum is a method we learned at Bank Street and is still practiced in schools.

I observed Wilbur's lanky frame, his lively blue eyes, and expressions fleeting across his face as he engaged with the children. They listened attentively, sometimes bursting into laughter. Not at all like my own schooldays sitting silently at a stationary desk, waiting for the teacher's instructions. With his good will, humor, and ability to communicate, Wilbur created a sense of trust and well-being in his classroom.

His enthusiasm was contagious, and, as we worked together, he awakened my imagination as well as my interest in learning the skills I needed to become a teacher. Soon I was contributing to the life of the classroom, and under Wilbur's tutelage, I was pouring paint into cups for the easel, reading stories to the children, and writing down the ones they told. I worked with small groups in reading and math instruction and studied nature on our frequent visits to Central Park, just around the corner from the school. I had never used a hammer or drilled holes before and was delighted to learn that one could create works of art with torn paper, fabric, sticks, or bottle-tops. Wilbur liked to recount how he realized we were kindred spirits when I brought in a wooden Venetian blind that I found on the street, and the children used it to make airplanes.

In contrast to me, brought up primarily in city environments, Wilbur was familiar with the outdoor life. Growing up in Nashville, he'd spent time in the Smoky Mountains, and a great deal of his education took place in informal settings outside of school. He roamed the woods with his friends, and they congregated in vacant lots, invented games, made toys, and learned nature lore from friendly neighbors.

Wilbur writes about these experiences:

◄ Much of our time was spent outdoors, just as children and youths have for centuries congregated in unsupervised groups, and despite an occasional fracas, some disputes and bullying, have met daily in free and easy discourse, give and take, with their own methods for resolving conflicts.

On our forays, we sometimes met our neighbor Mr. Quarles, and he shared with us his knowledge of nature lore. He might point to a tree or a plant and say: "Now that plant can be eaten if you are lost in the woods. Kinda bitter, a bit of onion grass improves the taste."

"Stop that," he once told me sternly as I was about to rub the rough fuzzy side of a Cow's Tongue leaf on the back of a kid's neck.

"The proper name," Mr. Quarles explained, "for that plant is Mullein. In colonial days, when rouge was hard to come by, country girls rubbed their cheeks with it before going out to square dances. It made their cheeks look rosy. Old folks boiled it down, made tea of it. Claimed it was good for ague and other ailments." ►

Origins and Inspiration

Working Together

I don't know if Wilbur ever found mullein growing in Central Park, but on our class visits there, we found sparkling mica-flecked stones to take back to school for art projects and further study. We explored the park's rock formations and observed the forms of tree barks and leaves. We watched and read about the behavior of squirrels, ducks, and pigeons. Sometimes Wilbur recounted stories of his early life, when he and his friends scrounged branches and discarded wood to make their own toys and hideaways. For our transportation unit, we collected the winged maple seeds, also known as whirly gigs. When we examined their structure, the kids discovered they were gummy and had fun sticking them on their noses. When they dropped the seeds out the window, we noted that their spiraling movements were similar to those of helicopters.

The class also took trips to observe the activities on the Hudson River and the harbor.

Back in school, Wilbur might ask:

◄ "What do you think was in the barge we saw being pulled by a tugboat?"

"Sand."

"Wood."

"Bananas." ►

They'd call out and Wilbur wrote the answers on a large sheet of lined paper. Of course, not everyone was interested in the happenings at the river; some remembered a dog they saw or the snack they ate.

Wilbur placed the completed "experience chart" where everyone could see it. It represented the children's thoughts and observations in their own familiar words that they practiced reading. They could do further research on questions, such as what barges carried, and consult books in the class library, as well as newspapers, magazines, and any relevant material we could find. They also drew and wrote or dictated their own interpretations of their trip.

Wilbur read books such as *The Little Engine That Could* to the group and encouraged the children to write their own stories. He was among the first people to record children's dictated stories and re-create them in homemade books that they could read. He listened

Wilbur and his class visit
the harbor.

Making music in Wilbur's
classroom.

Origins and Inspiration

carefully to what the children were saying, and the classroom was alive with conversation, word play, and puns.

His interest connected with my longtime love of stories and writing, and he inspired me to create stories for the children as well as help them with their own. Wilbur and his teaching embodied the concepts of Progressive Education that I was studying at Bank Street. He opened the door to a new world for me, and slowly we found ourselves drawn into it together.

Wilbur wrote about our relationship:

◄ Rachel and I were a good team. We found that we shared similar ideas about teaching and life and were interested in the arts. And some time after the school year ended, we took up residence together. Eventually we joined as co-teachers in the classroom of the Fifteenth Street School and continued our collaboration for the latter half of the 20th century. ►

I completed my studies at Bank Street, and for the next 10 years, Wilbur and I taught in separate schools. We relied on each other for advice about our teaching and spent much time discussing our experiences and school philosophies. For a brief time I was co-owner of a nursery school in Manhattan, but the administrative and financial responsibilities proved overwhelming. Wilbur and I continued dreaming of having our own school but felt stymied by the finances and all the complexities it would involve.

From Dream to Reality

When the tumultuous sixties arrived, young and old began expressing dissatisfaction and questioning the social conformity that characterized the fifties. After World War II, schools and educational policies came under scrutiny, and many educators disagreed about how to remedy the shortcomings in resources and pedagogy they perceived.

Rudolf Flesch's 1955 book *Why Johnny Can't Read* tried to deal with these issues and created much controversy. Flesch claimed that the problems in education would be resolved by changing reading methodologies from memorization of words (the "look-see" approach) to phonics instruction. This simple-minded panacea became the focus of the debate about education, which continued into the sixties and beyond.

While these controversies raged on, *Summerhill* was published in 1960, and Neill's philosophy of freedom resonated with the ethos of the time. Many "free" schools sprang up nationwide with the goal of giving children more of a voice in their own education. Each school developed its own interpretation of what comprised an ideal setting. We followed these events and felt hopeful with the new spirit in the air.

One day, Wilbur and I ran into a teacher we knew who told us she had heard that Orson Bean was planning to start a *Summerhill*-inspired school in New York City. We contacted Orson, and met him.

Wilbur wrote about our meeting:

◄ Our interest in working in the free school environment was longstanding and unrealized until we joined forces with Orson Bean, who announced that he planned to fund and operate a "Summerhill-type school." At the time, Orson was appearing in the Broadway play Never Too Late, and we met him between performances in a bar near the theater.

We found Orson to be personable and straightforward. He did not presume knowledge of the nitty-gritty of teaching, yet he was clear about the overarching nature of the school he envisioned. His intention was to have a setting where no compulsory studies were to be visited upon the students: a school in which children would have the opportunity to pursue their spirited lives in an environment responsive to their nature, their interests, and their desire to learn.

We talked about the unlikelihood that an urban day school could be modeled on Summerhill, a boarding school in a rural area. Still, I noted that it would be possible to adapt the more important features: self-regulation, children's choice of activities, absence of the usual controls and punishments, and if all went well, a lively, vital place.

Orson listened thoughtfully as we spoke about our experience and ideas and told us that he was going to look for a building in the Greenwich Village area. When all was said, he looked straight at us and told us we would make a good team.

Origins and Inspiration

A few days later we met again and agreed to work together to create the school. Here was the chance for Rachel and I to realize our longtime dream.

In this ideal arrangement for us, Orson would handle the financial and administrative work, and we would be in charge of the educational program. We looked forward to a productive partnership. ►

Orson purchased a building, formerly used by an offshoot of the teachers' union in the Chelsea area, just above Greenwich Village. Though today Chelsea is an upscale location, at the time it was a low-key residential and industrial neighborhood with a population of mixed income levels engaged in a variety of occupations.

Interaction Between Our School and the Neighborhood

What are now condos, boutiques, galleries, and restaurants were then printing houses, carpentry and car repair shops, lumberyards, and small factories producing clothing and upholstery. We could chat with the owners of stores such as Jimmy's Butcher Shop, Eugene's Cleaners, Ganbarg's Pharmacy, Laverty's Stationery, and the Farm Fresh Super Market.

Butler's Lumber Yard on Fourteenth Street was a special place. Throughout our years at the school, a teacher and some of the children regularly visited the yard. The fragrance of fresh sawdust greeted us as we entered the cavernous space, with its stacks of pine, plywood, and oak planks. We threaded our way around the whirring table saw in the middle of the floor, and the overall-clad workers cutting up boards.

"Do you have some scraps for our workbench?" we asked one of the lumbermen. He took us to a bin with odd wooden shapes and sometimes gave us larger pieces.

The school building on 15th Street,
ground floor remodled into a garage
by present owner.

Origins and Inspiration

"What do you think you'll make with this?" he might wonder.

"Maybe a plane or a truck. We'll bring you something we made. Thanks a lot." We waved goodbye and, with our plastic bags filled with the gifts of these hearty, good-willed men, headed back to school.

Also of interest was Hy and Mel's Luncheonette, only a few doors from the school. At first, the brothers' luncheonette seemed like a casual drop-in place, but over time it grew to be a vital part of our environment. Because it was so close, the elementary-age kids were able to go there on their own to purchase lunch or snacks.

Behind a long narrow counter, Hy and Mel, along with their helper, prepared sodas, malteds, sandwiches, tea, and coffee. At the cash register near the entrance, they sold magazines, cigarettes, cookies, and candies, displayed in boxes and racks. The luncheonette was a neighborhood hub, a forum where young and old chatted about sports and politics, observed the passing scene, and listened to the brothers' tales of the latest happenings in the area. The children read signs and menus and browsed through comics. Hy and Mel liked the kids and invited them to assist in dispensing sodas, making sandwiches and malteds, and collecting money. What could be better?!

Under Hy and Mel's matter-of-fact tutelage, the children expanded their skills in math, in working cooperatively, in service to others, and in taking responsibility. They exercised their competence and earned due respect for the work they performed. All were peers in this seamless, pleasurable setting, and we welcomed this serendipitous extension of our school. It provided opportunities for informal learning in a real-life setting.

Years later, Hy and Mel were honored with a special tribute in the gym/auditorium. They reflected on their relationships with the children:

Mel: I think that one day we just let the kids help out at the cash register, and then another one asked, and how could you refuse? In the classroom the children are somewhat removed from society; here they can see how it all works.

Hy: Sometimes I think it's almost like we're giving a course in cash registering. The kids are good kids and their coming here during lunch hour breaks up the day for us.

Voices of Children

Hy *(left)* and Mel.

Allan.

Origins and Inspiration

Hy and Mel were truly community workers, part of the multitude of natural mentors who enrich our world. Alas, the luncheonette fell victim to gentrification and raised rents and was replaced by a nail parlor.

Allan Converse, a graduate, recently told me that, "I still remember that place and those two guys very fondly. I think it is a shame that kids growing up in this neighborhood now will have no appreciation at all for how ordinary people live and work."

In this milieu of the old Chelsea neighborhood, we began our work to shape the spacious building into our school.

The Social Context of the 1960's

In his popular song, "The Times They Are A-changin'," Bob Dylan reflected on the changing world of the 1960's when our school opened. The Vietnam War raged abroad, and at home, Wilbur and I joined demonstrations to protest it. We supported the Civil Rights and Women's Liberation Movements' struggles for equality and justice in all spheres of life and were horrified by the violence and hatred with which they were being met. Numbers of young people known as hippies rejected their comfortable lifestyles and sought to establish their own "counterculture" based on the values of love, peace, freedom, and artistic expression, removed from the strictures of commercial enterprise.

Most people, now with access to TV, watched broad news coverage on their home screens. The Vietnam conflict was the first time that a war was viewed in real time, and the children were aware of these events. In school, we discussed what was happening in the world.

In colleges, students staged sit-ins, demanding more participation in school affairs, and in academic circles, the very notion of compulsory schooling came into question. In fact, in many rural and non-industrial societies, children are not separated from their families to learn survival skills. They learn alongside their parents and elders, sometimes in peer groups. They spend much of their time outdoors, engaged in motor activity, or in the home, learning essential tasks. They learn "on the job" what is required to live in their society.

Barbara Rogoff (2014) observed how Mayan children in Mexico learn intricate skills by participating in ongoing family and community endeavors. They learn by collaborating with adults in sharing tasks, such as weaving and planting, while adults help children to master skills through gradual steps appropriate to each child's level. Rogoff calls this "learning by observing and pitching in" and contrasts this method to children being isolated in a building and taught through prepared materials they must memorize and repeat.

Peter Gray (2013) has written about the largely self-directed life of children in hunting-gathering societies. With local materials, they build huts and toys, and their games consist of dramatic play, such as acting as trackers, hunters, or arbitrators: scenarios relating to life in their society. They spend most of their time in peer groups, and their conduct is accepted and respected by adults. Through their play, they learn to emulate the activities and absorb the concepts required for functioning in their settings and to eventually undertake adult tasks. Gray and Rogoff have described examples of cultures that respect children as independent learners, where adults intuitively foster the children's inclinations to learn the skills they need to function. These views are in line with those of thinkers such as Rousseau, Tolstoy, Froebel, Homer Lane, A.S. Neill, John Dewey, Vygotsky, and others who grasped the notion that children need interactive, supportive environments in which to develop.

Alison Gopnick, an American professor of psychology and affiliate professor of philosophy at the University of California, Berkeley, wrote that "We don't have to make children learn; we just have to let them learn."

In the 1970s, the American educator/author John Holt propounded the concept of education outside of school structures. From years of teaching and observing, he concluded that schools engendered fear in children and were inimical to their development. He believed that in a stimulating environment, children would learn what they were ready to learn when they were ready to learn it. Gradually, some parents began to educate their children at home, and, coalescing around

Origins and Inspiration

Holt's concept of unschooling, the Home Schooling Movement was born. (You can read more about this in chapter 8.)

During that period of ferment, even the public school system incorporated new ideas. Some schools adapted variations of progressive educational methodology and others adopted the new British pedagogy of the Open Classroom. In this system, students worked independently at learning stations with materials prepared by the teachers. Another change occurred due to over-crowding, and public schools spun off neighborhood satellites, often in storefronts. In these somewhat independent units, teachers enjoyed a high degree of autonomy.

Reflecting on this time of change and evolution, Wilbur wrote in an article called "The Legacy of Paul Goodman" in the periodical *Change* (1972–73).

Here is an excerpt:

◄ There are lots of things going on that we're not aware of. For example, there are a lot of little storefront schools connected to a public school up in East Harlem. They are in a little shopping center or alongside a public housing development; they have kindergarten and some first grades. They've been running for a few years and they are beautiful. There is a lot of space; the teachers are free from all the pressure of those big buildings and their bureaucracies, though they are still affected by it. And they run very neat, humane programs for the children. There is that contact with the people in the street— the postman comes in, you know, the kids are constantly involved in the ordinary daily activities of their communities. And it's lively. ►

These innovations have mostly been jettisoned in favor of scripted, test-oriented curricula, though at this time an increasing number of parents and teachers are rejecting the current trends in public education. Many are turning to alternatives such as The Albany Free School (founded in 1969), the Brooklyn Free School, the Manhattan Agile Learning Center, the Sudbury Valley Schools, and others practicing Democratic Education. The schools vary in their methodologies. For example, the Sudbury Valley School (founded in 1968) has eschewed scheduled classes and teacher-directed curricula, and students and mentors develop their own learning experiences. At the

Agile Learning Center, teachers develop tools to help the children articulate their interests and find ways to realize and reflect on them. The group AERO (Alternative Education Resource Organization) acts as a network for communication among these, as well as more than two hundred similar schools worldwide, and the Alliance for Self-Directed Education promotes the concept through publications on its website.

Though the sixties were a time of broad social unrest, with movements expressing dissatisfaction and demands for change in all aspects of society, it was also a time of innovation and creativity in education, social life, and the arts. At the Fifteenth Street School, we incorporated some of the new, emerging art forms. Improvisational theater and the revived crafts movement, with its colorful tie-dyes and emphasis on non-commercial handmade objects, found their way into our classroom. All age groups listened to the protest songs of Bob Dylan and other original groups.

Wilbur and I read Rachel Carson's *Silent Spring*, published in 1962, and were dimly aware of the beginnings of a movement to preserve the planet. The children reflected this interest in the environment in their imaginative construct they called The Farm of the Six, a projection of an idyllic future life of cooperation on an ideal farm.

The world of technology was expanding rapidly. Computers, extended TV viewing, jet travel, missiles, and space exploration altered the perception of space and time. The children incorporated the daring events they witnessed in space explorations by building a launching pad with blocks and creating scenarios such as First Guinea to Land on the Moon.

Our doors opened almost a year after the assassination of President John F. Kennedy. The murders of Martin Luther King, Jr. and presidential candidate Bobby Kennedy occurred a few years later. When Lyndon Johnson won the presidency in 1964, a majority of parents at the school opposed the war and expressed sympathy for his Great Society platform. Wilbur and I shared these views but were careful not to impose them on the children. Over time, they found their own creative interpretations of these events through their imaginary campaigns and elections of Troll and Guinea Pig mayors and presidents. These campaigns were metaphors for events in the world,

Origins and Inspiration

Election poster.

Voices of Children

and the children developed their own Problem-Solving Committee to deal with problems in the school. In this time of turmoil and heightened energy, our group felt remarkably calm as we worked on developing the Fifteenth Street School.

Getting Started with Students, Parents, and Staff

When *Summerhill* was published in the United States in 1960, Neill's ideas were in sync with the segment of our society seeking changes from constraining authority. A sizeable audience read the book, and Orson spoke about it and his plan for the Fifteenth Street School on the TV game show *To Tell the Truth*. News about Orson's school spread by word of mouth, and a number of parents contacted him to request interviews. Some were familiar with Neill's philosophy, and some were drawn to the idea that their children could learn and pursue their own initiatives with the guidance of knowledgeable, experienced adults. Orson had also been involved with the Summerhill Society, and some applicants came through them.

Orson made appointments for us to visit the families in their homes. The newness of it all made us feel a bit tense, and we did our best to answer their questions about our experience and ideas for the school. We, too, had questions about the children's lives and interests, their previous schooling, and the parents' expectations. Some of the children had attended pre-school programs, and for the six-year-olds, it would be their first experience in elementary school.

The socio-economic makeup of the student body was typical for independent schools of the time. There were no scholarships at our school, and those who could afford the fees were mostly professionals, artists, or business people. There was no attempt to recruit students from diverse backgrounds, and just one African-American family enrolled their daughter.

After the interviews, some parents felt confident enough to enroll their children in our school, though it did not yet exist. Orson's upbeat personality and our straightforward manner made us seem a credible team. I see now that everyone—parents, students, and staff alike—had a great deal of courage entering into an unknown enterprise. We felt optimistic as we plunged into the work ahead. Wilbur and I had both worked in traditional and progressive schools, and from these, our readings, and our childhoods and youth, a view of the child's life and learning emerged. We hoped to create a school different from established schooling, in significant ways, both theoretically and practically.

An experienced early-childhood teacher joined our team, and our founding group, consisting of Orson and the staff, began planning from scratch. We scheduled our meetings as needed and worked well together. Being involved in creating something new and meaningful filled us with energy.

We began by establishing the basic administrative structure. Orson would be the school's director and business manager, and Wilbur would direct the educational program. Among other things, Wilbur was to be responsible for working with state officials to obtain accreditation for the school, and Orson set the tuition in line with current private school fees.

We decided to begin with two separate age groups, though children of different ages could mix freely. The early-childhood teacher and an assistant worked with the four- and five-year-olds on the second floor, and Wilbur and I were in charge of the elementary age group on the third floor. With these in place, we hammered out our operating procedures, as well as the concepts to guide us.

Forging Our Philosophy and Pedagogy

The staff, with Orson, considered the basic philosophy of our school. How would it compare to the conventional and progressive schools we were familiar with? Along with Neill, we rejected the conventional school model with its uniformity, rigid scheduling, rote learning, and lock-step authority. From Progressive Education, we drew on the concept of interactive learning by which students construct knowledge by interacting with their environment and each other, using educational materials, and valuing creative expression and cordial relationships between students and teachers.

We thought about Summerhill, which is often referred to as a free school. The term "free school" denotes a place where children have leeway in where and how to spend their time and are not required to attend scheduled classes or take exams to measure their progress. Detractors often claim that free schools lead to anarchy and license. They imagine a permissive atmosphere where the worst instincts flourish: laziness, bullying, inability to concentrate and learn—all causing children to become social misfits unable to find employment. Neill used the phrase "freedom not license" to distinguish between the freedom from restraints that inhibit growth and irresponsible self-indulgence. He wrote about the work required to live in a community where children exert choice in directing their lives.

Neill evolved his pedagogy in reaction to the rigid, punitive schooling he experienced, first as a student, then as a teacher. In the post–World War I era, he came in contact with new ideas about life, which led him to form his philosophy about education. It was the time of Freud's recent theories about human nature and the unconscious. It was the time that artists and educators saw children as independent learners, and as artists creating their own meaningful images. It was the time of Progressive Education in the United States and of the New Jersey Stelton Modern School based on the principles of the anarchist educator Francisco Ferrer. Neill worked with the educator Homer Lane, from whose pioneering, non-punitive approach with delinquents he formed his belief in children's inherent striving for growth.

When Neill visited schools in Germany, he joined the innovative International School (*Neue Schule Hellerau*) where he was moved by witnessing the children's expressive dance movements in the Dalcroze School's Eurhythmy program. When Neill gave a lecture at a conference in Salzburg, he was excited to hear Franz Cizek talk about his revolutionary art school in Vienna, where he encouraged children to represent their own ideas. And earlier, in 1861, Tolstoy had inspired his students at his free school at Yasnaya Polyana to write their own stories, which he deemed superior to his own. Neill grasped that children possessed self-generating capacities that would

Origins and Inspiration

flourish in an environment that encouraged imaginative play and where children could create in their own time and space. In 1921, he set up his first trial school at Hellerau, where children could develop their own dramatic scenarios, music, dance, art, and craft. "An out and out 'doing" school,'" he stated. In 1926 he followed this model with Summerhill in England.

Neill did not expect specific learning to result from play and did not think that games or equipment should be used as learning aids. He stated, "Childhood is not adulthood. Childhood is play-hood and no child ever gets enough play. I am not decrying learning, but learning should come after play. And learning should not deliberately be seasoned with play to make it palatable."

For learning reading, math, and other skills, Neill and his staff set up conventional instructional classes. Each child signed up for classes and received a timetable. Neill unconditionally affirmed the children's right to decide how to spend their time. They could work in the art and craft studios, play on their own, and/or attend instructional classes. He was confident that in a school setting where children could roam, explore, and build safely, they would want to gain skills and knowledge and attend formal classes. Neill unabashedly asserted that the goal of education was happiness, by which he meant being interested, engaged.

He wrote, "We set out to make a school in which we should allow children freedom to be themselves. In order to do this, we had to renounce all discipline, all direction, all suggestion, all moral training, all religious instruction. We have been called brave, but it did not require courage. All it required was what we had—a complete belief in the child as a good, not an evil, being. Since 1921 this belief in the goodness of the child has never wavered; rather, it has become a final faith."

He worked with many children who could not adjust to the conventional school system where they developed attitudes of mistrust, and, sometimes, destructive behavior. Though Neill's method did not work for everyone, his faith was reaffirmed by the many who recovered and thrived at Summerhill.

It is nearly a century since Neill first sought to make his school into a "self-governing democracy," and in 2006 the author/educator

Ron Miller reviewed Neill's ideas in his book *The Directory of Democratic Education.* His definition articulates the concept that guided us at the Fifteenth Street School.

"Democratic Education is an educational approach," he said, "grounded in respect for human rights and a broad interpretation of learning in which young people have the freedom to organize their daily activities, and in which there is equality and democratic decision-making among young people and adults."

Our staff agreed that, though we were inspired by Neill's philosophy, our school would not be a duplicate of Summerhill. Our challenge was to draw on our experience and research to create a day school for our students of that time and place.

Over our years of teaching, Wilbur and I marveled at the intensity and originality children demonstrated in their spontaneous play. Based on our observations of how children learned through their play with materials—wood, paint, clay, found objects—their dramatic scenarios; singing and dancing; language; and social interactions, we were able to use our own creativity to support and expand their abilities. At the Fifteenth Street School, we planned for teachers and students to work together on emerging ideas from which learning could grow in suitable time frames. We used methods of instruction from progressive education, while following Neill's philosophy of greater freedom and self-determination.

Wilbur wrote about the environment we aimed to develop:

◄ A free school requires adults who are responsive to children's specific needs and interests, who can nurture their inherent urges to learn, with both child and adult engaged and participating in the learning process. The adults must be knowledgeable about and promote and develop the children's lives: their expressions, their movements, their motivations, their interests and capacities.

The environment must support the children's interest in becoming competent in the skills of the culture as well as cultivating the self-reflective capacity that governs rational behavior. They will have access to materials and structures to learn the basic tool skills.

Origins and Inspiration

The relationships formed with peers and with teachers often determine how children are regarded – as creatures living, working and playing in the context of a specific developmental arena. At this age (6-8) powerful formative familial and social experiences await them, and yet their own childhood is splendid with pliability and versatility. ►

With these thoughts in mind, we proceeded to work on setting up the school.

Planning for Time and Space

We thought about how the space in the building could be used to create a safe learning environment for active minds and bodies, a place where children could find the materials and support to stimulate their innate interest in learning. We had all taught in self-contained classrooms where children could not leave the room without the teacher's permission, and we planned to have no restrictions on the children's movements within the classrooms. However, Orson, with his common sense and intuitive trust of children, went further and insisted that they be allowed to move through the building at will. Despite our concerns about safety and questions about maintaining cohesive groups for instruction, we agreed to try it.

For us, this was a radical departure from our way of working with scheduled programs in defined spaces. It created a new dynamic in our relationship to space, time, and authority. Children would not be compelled to stay in one room, sustain any one activity, or be supervised at all times. They would control the time they spent in spaces of their own choosing and have access to a variety of environments and personal connections during each day. We planned to present these ideas to the children in the first days of school.

Teachers would take time to observe the rhythms and interests of the children in action, and to speak with them and each other about how it all worked. They would develop ideas and structures suitable to the students' needs based on the emerging patterns they observed and find ways to safeguard everyone's rights and well-being.

Voices of Children

Origins and Inspiration

Because the students could choose when to attend any activity, the program would differ significantly from the progressive format where children are responsible for participating in the class study of a central theme (the Harbor, Transportation, or Early Life in New York, for example) and follow a somewhat flexible schedule in a designated space.

Wilbur's thoughts about time and space in our school:

◄ In a free school, time has no resemblance to the factory model's rigid encapsulations. Time in a free school is fluid within the context of the adult's goals in furthering basic skills —reading, writing, and math, the arts, and the experimentation that furthers inquiry in the sciences. An integral part of any educator's approach to young children carefully examines who controls the children's use of time and space and how that control is communicated.

At the Fifteenth Street School, the schedule of the day is such that children can determine how to spend their time. This does not mean that the teacher is inoperative, for at such times, he/she may either initiate an activity in some area with a group of children or be called upon by the children as a resource and thereby become engaged in their self-initiated activities. At other times, the teacher may be present, observing, reacting, available. ►

In this fluid setting, the staff needed to be vigilant and responsive, as children and teachers collaborated in the conduct of school life. With an entire building at our disposal and a commitment to giving the children the freedom to explore it, we began to allocate spaces and equip them with materials. We made decisions about use of space that framed what would take place there.

Designing a Layout and Choosing Equipment

Wilbur described our goals:

◄ We aimed to create an environment characterized by a mutuality of effort between the children and adults in the time/space most conducive to learning, with the most felicitous availability of suitable materials. ►

We worked on allocating the space in the four-story building and thought that the ground floor was ideal for a free play area. Since we had already designated the second and third floor for different age groups, that meant the fourth floor, which had no formal use, could become a classroom for another group as the school expanded. The roof was fenced in, and small decks on the third and fourth floors afforded outdoor play areas as well.

While the building was being cleaned and painted, we selected the equipment we needed. With the exception of the ground floor, we set up the rooms in the style of the progressive classrooms we were familiar with. Orson left the staff to select appropriate materials from available catalogues and generously financed these purchases. We ordered child-scaled tables and chairs, and Wilbur made low shelves that we stocked with books, puzzles, Lego, and Tic Tac Toe, plus reading and math materials, such as Cuisenaire Rods and small blocks. The children could use these at any time, as well as design their own images from "raw materials" (aka "loose parts"), such as paper, pencils, crayons, wood, clay, and paints. We also purchased some percussion instruments and a mimeograph machine: the hand-operated copier of its time.

In the past, we had often worked with limited resources and tried to find free materials for our classrooms. It was a challenge to find a print or upholstery shop and convince them to donate scrap paper or fabric for the children's projects. We befriended liquor and appliance store workers and collected cardboard boxes and appliance containers that became dwellings. The concept of recycling was not yet in popular use, and many materials were disposed of in the garbage.

At Bank Street, Lois Lord, a pioneering art teacher working in an experimental children's art program at the Museum of Modern Art, taught us how to improvise collages and 3D constructions with paper and "found objects." We also learned from the arts of Africa and the works of modern artists such as Picasso and Kurt Schwitters, who transformed discarded materials into meaningful objects. We learned from the kids as well, and eventually we even tried our own hands at creating artworks.

Origins and Inspiration

To our school, we brought clothing and hats for dramatic play and some of our collection of machines, such as gears, pulleys, small car parts, radio and TV circuits, and old telephones. The kids could use these as imaginary props for dramatic play and take them apart for their constructions. The inside of a radio was a potential space transmission station, and TV circuitry panels could be parts of motors.

Wilbur wrote about the equipment he made in his workshop:

◄ In the school basement I made shelving, easels, games, platforms for dramatic play, a workbench, and "kitchen" appliances for the younger group. From my favorite junk/antiques dealer in Woodstock, I got the insides of an old gasoline pump that had all kinds of gears and numerals the kids could twirl around. They liked to use this kind of thing as a prop for their scenarios. ►

We now felt privileged to have the space and materials afforded to us, but we would always collect corks, bottle-tops, coffee stirrers, fabric buttons, cardboard, wood, and boxes to be recycled into collections for sorting and counting and transformed by the children's imaginations.

The "Gym"

With children not being required to stay in their classrooms, we needed alternate spaces in which they could spend their time. At Summerhill and other schools in country settings, children have access to outdoor spaces where they can play and exercise large muscles. At our school, the room running from front to back on the ground floor had the makings of an indoor yard. This cavernous space with a plain linoleum-covered floor and a large window at one end came to be called the gym.

Wilbur described how it was used:

◄ Consider the setting on the ground floor of the school, a large room approximately 20 feet by 80 feet. The children call this space the gym, although it has no traditional floor markings or basketball hoops or other gym paraphernalia.

Voices of Children

At one end of the space is a raised platform. The equipment includes large fiber drum-shaped containers holding foam blocks and used as dwellings, hideouts, and spaceships; some sturdy wheel toys; various and assorted adult clothes, alpaca coat linings, and a strange assortment of headwear; cardboard boxes in varied stages of collapse and climbing bars with foam pads underneath. A friend of the school donated a working jukebox whose lively music was used as accompaniment for some of the children's shows. In a built-in closet, we stored folding chairs for special events such as sing-ins, holiday parties, and children's dramatic and musical presentations. And that is it.

This space makes no demands; it is there for the taking, and what happens within it must be created by the children's movement and imagination. All children in school, once it is known that they are able to handle themselves in terms of safety, are allowed to go to the gym at any time. The gym area is not supervised continuously, though teachers check to see that there is no major friction, or simply to be au courant of what is happening. The children here are free from the impingement of adult consciousness.

In essence, the children can do what they please. Now, as surprising as it may seem, they don't tear up the place, deface the walls, place themselves in dangerous situations, or engage in frenzied onslaughts upon each other. Considering the amount of time the gym is in use by small groups of children, only a modicum of time is required of the adults to settle arguments or to define territory. Children come and go freely; playgroups are the result of common interests. There is no problem as a group of four-year-olds act out a family story in their informal dramatic play in one area, while a group of six-year-old children explore balancing and rolling on barrels from an upright position in another.

One of the reasons that the children don't do silly or inappropriate things when they are not directly supervised, apart from their general good sense, is because we assume that they are more able to take care of themselves than is commonly believed. In this assumption is the breeding ground for furthering the sense of self-worth, self-trust, and competency that in turn reinforces rational behavior.

In planning the school, the staff thought of the gym (as well as the two enclosed roof areas available with play equipment), as an appropriate area for large motor movements for boisterous, noisy behavior, and for what might be called purposeless play. Purposeless in the sense of play that is not content-oriented or directed, but purposeful in the sense that the children's need for release of energy in vigorous ways of their own choice is affirmed.

During our four years at the school, one accident occurred in the gym: A girl lost her balance on the climbing bars and fell against a tub below. She suffered a slight injury. We examined all the gym equipment and made adjustments, and of course, we questioned the whole gym experience. After discussing this and talking with parents and children, we decided to continue the program and keep a more frequent check on the gym and the arrangement of the equipment.

The children used the gym for a wide variety of formal and informal games. Formal included rule-bound activities like stoop-tag, freeze-tag, tug-of-war, modified baseball, and circle games like London Bridge Is Falling Down. Informal games assume more loosely structured forms of dramatic play, such as playing "space" (astronauts in outer space) or household play, informal dance and movement, and wrestling, chasing, running, skipping, and hugging. In a sense, an area such as this works somewhat like the backyard or vacant lot of our rural backgrounds or like the city street or playground, where children play games like those children have always played—games they organize and monitor on their own. ►

After visiting the Fifteenth Street School, George Leonard wrote in his book *Education and Ecstasy* (1968), that, "It is instructive to spend a day in the gym. As children come and go, the mood of the place shifts like a summer sky. Boisterous pursuit runs its course, subsides into a time of watching and waiting. A child turns out the lights, and the only illumination filters in through windows at the

At the jukebox in the gym.

Origins and Inspiration

far end. Now the gym is a cavern of silence and mystery. The senses become acute. Children are aware of each other, their movements, their feelings. A new group enters. Someone turns on the jukebox. Everything changes. With the freedom to do so, why don't children spend all their time in the gym? The question would naturally occur to most of us, whose school experience has consisted of sitting long hours at teachers' commands, of repeating the same thing over and over again, of wishing and waiting to escape. Children at Fifteenth Street leave the gym because their bodies and minds tell them they have had enough, and because other fascinating and deeply involving educational environments are available."

The gym was a blank canvas on which the children used their imaginations freely. They daydreamed and improvised plays and acrobatic and musical shows they performed for their peers. They interacted with each other and experienced excitement, pleasure, disappointment, anger, and joy. The gym put an important aspect of the school's philosophy into action and is remembered fondly by some of the graduates as one of its salient features.

The Second Floor: Four and Five-Year-Olds and the School Office

Here, in a large room with windows facing the street, the teachers set up the space for the four- and five-year-old group. It contained child-sized tables and chairs; a block-building area; a place for dramatic play, including a kitchen area with a scaled wooden sink, refrigerator and small bed, plastic cookware, and a variety of dress-up clothes. Also available: an easel with paints, shelves with books and table games, puzzles and materials for drawing, clay, and plasticene. The children chose their activities and assisted by their teachers, moved freely in the large open room. At times, they went to play in the gym or visit "the big kids" on the third floor.

Staging a spacewalk in the gym.

Margaret, students and dogs
in her office.

Origins and Inspiration

Down the hall, Margaret, the school secretary, and her resident Chihuahua always kept an open door for visitors to her cozy office. Warm-hearted Margaret, with her down-to-earth manner and her desk and books, provided a comforting presence. The kids were always welcome to drop in for a chat, vent problems, play with the dog, read, draw, relax, and occasionally watch programs on the TV set installed in the room. When the early NASA space shots were televised, the children crowded round the set to watch. Being in Margaret's office was somewhat like visiting a favorite aunt you could confide in.

The Third Floor: Six-Year-Olds, the Wood Room, and the Art Room

Wilbur and I worked on the third floor, starting with a group of approximately 15 six-year-olds. The floor was comprised of two large rooms (the Wood Room and the Art Room) separated by a hallway, a kitchen, a coatroom, and a small room for special projects. A small deck, overlooking backyards, extended from the Art Room.

Wilbur mostly presided in the Wood Room, a large space facing Fifteenth Street. We furnished it with a workbench, tools, and shelves with building blocks. On one side Wilbur built a narrow platform for dramatic play, and on another wall we hung grocery-store posters advertising items on sale. We thought the children would relate to familiar symbols they had seen in shops, as well as to the common machine parts we had assembled. Wilbur's presence and energy, the tools, and machinery attracted many of the boys, though the girls also used the tools and built with blocks (for more on this topic, see the section on building in chapter 6).

I spent most of my time in the Art Room, at the opposite end of the hall from the Wood Room. Here, children worked with readily accessible art materials, read books from the class library, used table games, and dressed up with hats and clothes for dramatic play. They could relax in comfortable seating and lounging areas with cushions

Making life-sized constructions
with various-size blocks.

Origins and Inspiration

and blankets, read, chat, or listen to records of folk songs by Woody Guthrie and Pete Seeger, and the exciting new music of the Beatles and the Mamas & the Papas, loved by young and old. They played instruments and accompanied songs they made up. We introduced plants and animals for enjoyment and as subjects of study. The art and wood rooms had areas furnished with age-scaled tables and chairs and could be used for discussions and individual and group instruction. The building, with its varied spaces, child-oriented furnishings, and equipment, was a concrete representation of the environment we envisioned to implement our philosophy: a place for children to inhabit and make their own.

Origins and Inspiration

From an evolutionary perspective,
play is nature's way of ensuring that children and young mammals
learn what they must to survive and do well.

– Peter Gray

Chapter 2

The School in Action

In addition to the decisions we made about personnel and the use of space, we considered how to allocate time. School started and ended at regular times, and we worked on finding time frames to accommodate the evolving flow of activities. Interactions among children and between children and teachers brought our philosophy to life.

Creating Informal and Formal Schedules

After school opened, we took time to observe how the children directed themselves before deciding when and how to introduce topics of interest. On a typical day, the children arrived at different times, some by bus and the rest from the neighborhood. They checked into their classroom and chatted with their friends, fed the guinea pigs, took up their ongoing projects, read, drew, built, or went to the gym. They worked and played on their own, in self-selected groups, or attended a teacher-initiated activity. Wilbur and I had plans for introducing activities like science experiments, painting, puppetry, trips, and storytelling. We called for meetings as needed, to announce the schedule, share stories, hear individual complaints, or discuss school issues such as kids disrupting a group trying to concentrate.

We stayed in touch with the pulse of the group and its changing atmosphere as the day wore on. Midafternoon was often a time when children's energies waned, and we would consult with each other and decide how to proceed. It might be a good time for a story or to go to the roof. The roof was the one place in the building where, for safety reasons, the children could not go by themselves. As the school day approached its end, we apprised the kids of the time and tried to engage them in putting the rooms in order. Though they would return to their projects and pursuits the next day, many were loath to leave.

We were concerned with the learning of basic skills (reading/math) and developing structures that would ensure the children's mastery. We decided to set up an informal schedule with groups meeting at a regular time each day to work on these skills. The children could work independently or with a teacher, and we remained a constant presence to assist with their evolving projects and ideas. It is hard to reconstruct exactly how and when activities were initiated, by whom they were introduced, or how long they lasted.

Wilbur had specific thoughts about scheduling:

◄ It seems that rigidly enforcing program-learning schemes with young children severs them from some important life potentials, even when the narrow goal of the program is realized. There is no doubt that scheduling in human affairs is at times a benefit. At the Fifteenth Street School, some events, like classes, trips or visitors, were scheduled for necessary management reasons. We did not assume that children would always participate but thought that some would be interested in attending, and generally they were.

Children brought their own lunch and could eat when they chose and go to the bathroom when they felt the need. They decided when and how long to socialize with peers, be alone, or with an adult. This fluidity, this intentional absence of rigid, mandatory participation in all matters, ranging from classes to relationships, established an atmosphere of orderly freedom. We were prepared to move with the flow of events and took advantage of the fortuitous, and of the emerging interests shown by the children. For instance, we'd issue a call throughout the school on any given day that a show or story time was going to take place in half an hour, and suddenly, all the children would come to witness it.

When making choices, it's not so much a matter of either/or as the richness of possibility. ►

The Rhythms of Child-Initiated Activities

Though dealing with children moving freely in their school environment was new for us, we found that their movement in and out of rooms, up and down the stairs, took on its own organic form, somewhat like the rhythm of tides. We relaxed and were able to adapt to the ebbs and flows of their energies. The four teachers took responsibility to check the gym throughout the day on a non-scheduled, spontaneous basis. Sometimes, one of us would spend time there to facilitate the children's work with plays, music, and acrobatics or discuss news or family events.

Wilbur noted his ideas about the significance of movement:

◄ Movement is intrinsic to life. Its expression in rational human behavior occurs in concert with the physical, the emotional, and the cerebral as a totality, rather than as is often thought, in a mechanical separation of operations. When young children are free to move from one activity to another according to their own volition and interest, we find not a constant restless parade, but an orderly pattern of movement.

Using large, expansive movements, the children play vigorously in the gym or on the enclosed roof. They play games, run, chase, shout and dance and sing. After a while, and the time duration varies from day to day and child to child, there is an inevitable and voluntary return to the more concentrated activities of the classroom. They are ready to regulate their movements and sounds in keeping with quiet activities.

Children are creatures not only of exuberance, but also of intensity, seriousness and silence. This is not to say that thinking takes place only after vigorous exercise or when we are physically energetic. Minds are as varied as the bodies that house them. Each mind, each body has an energetic rhythm of its own, and we should be wary of prescribing one way for the mind to work. What is clear is that a classroom wherein vigorous bodies are compulsorily fixed at desks or tables for undue periods of time has an adverse effect on the energetic system. Such an environment dulls the mind and reinforces daydreaming of the student and the inertia of the teacher. ►

The School in Action

top & bottom: Activities on
school balconies.

Voices of Children

Views of the School: Feedback and Assessment

Though there was always a lot of energy, sounds of voices, children expressing emotions, laughing and singing, the children were able to regulate their behavior without disturbances for the most part.

We conducted our school day in a decentralized style and, after school hours, Wilbur and I reviewed what had taken place. We evaluated how the structure was working and made plans for the functioning of the group. As we did not have a central group theme that everyone related to, we had to decide how to introduce new content and expand on the children's emerging interests. We needed to find suitable activities for children who had come to us from other schools and had to get used to the school format.

To assist the students in becoming competent in the skills, we reviewed each one's work to determine what kind of help he or she needed. Based on our observations and assessments, we made changes, reinforced the things that were working, and grappled with ideas to follow up. We created worksheets for reading and math and purchased equipment when needed.

The proximity of parents made their concerns a constant part of our daily landscape. Although they generally subscribed to the school philosophy and methodology, many were anxious to have their children perform close to grade level in the basic skills of reading and math. We held conferences to talk about their children and address their questions. Not every problem had a solution, and several families withdrew their children from the school for various reasons.

For most of the children, this was their first elementary school experience, and they accepted the setting as conventional. The informality of the school, and the continuous face-to-face interactions, created the conditions for the positive teacher/student collaboration that developed.

The teachers for the two groups and Orson worked in an informal, supportive atmosphere and held meetings as the need arose. While continuing his acting/TV career, Orson managed to spend a good amount of time at the school, dealing with administrative matters and sometimes doing magic shows. He was a vital presence and his upbeat, positive energy and humor acted as a welcome tonic.

The School in Action

I remember that in the days and weeks after our school opened, we all congratulated ourselves on how well everything was proceeding. Yet, despite all our experience, studies, beliefs, and collegiality, we were all stepping on terra incognita. Excited as we were, we were also anxious about how this would play out.

Wilbur's notes underscore some of our concerns:

◄ We strove for an environment supporting the young child's drives for pleasure, freedom of movement, opportunity to explore and learn about the world, to become competent in the skills of the culture, to be independent. Our question was: given that the disciplining modes were other than those generally practiced in schools, and eschewing practices such as verbal and physical abuse and moralistic admonitions, as well as permissiveness, i.e., "doing anything you want," what would be the responses of young children? ►

Philosophies of Behavior and Governance

In every type of school, the issue of behavior and governance is central. How a school manages behavior and governance depends upon the school's basic philosophical tenets.

Conventional education follows the philosophy that regards children as empty vessels, into which the school systematically transmits a common set of skills and knowledge. To subdue the active nature of children, teachers make them sit at desks most of the time, following rigid schedules and common standards of behavior. Children are expected to obey school rules unconditionally and on frequent tests must try to duplicate the information they have been given.

The Progressive philosophy recognizes the active nature of children as participants in their own development and learning process and provides a structured arena for its expression and growth. Teachers create interactive environments where students can learn from each other and the world around them. Children engage in free movement within a defined framework and are encouraged to express their creativity and develop their thinking skills. The staff

Guinea pig goes to reading class.

The School in Action

maintains a cordial environment, explains behavioral expectations, and adjudicates conflicts in a non-punitive manner.

The free or democratic school philosophy regards children as independent agents capable of directing their own learning process and provides an open-ended arena where they can grow and find expression. Benign adults assist them to function and learn in their own ways, in their own time. Teachers and children collaborate to develop and enforce standards of behavior.

During a typical school day, at all types of schools, students and teachers experience a wide range of interactions and express a gamut of emotions. Each environment will determine what is accepted, what must be modified, and what is rejected.

Based on his experience, Neill came to believe that living organisms have a propensity to set their own terms for constructively meeting and governing their needs. His vision set a new standard in the area of understanding and regulating behavior. At Summerhill, Neill developed a supportive environment to nurture children's capacity for self-regulation. To deal rationally with conflicts, he set up a governing body run jointly by staff and students. Everyone was encouraged to attend a weekly "General School Meeting" where children explained and discussed their problems. Students ran the meetings as rotating chairpersons, and student enforcers or ombudsmen were on call to deal with problems at all times. They brought complaints to the group for discussion and judgments, which sometimes included mild sanctions, such as being excluded from a trip or dessert.

Children learned to practice democratic governance by working together to shape expectations of behavior and the ethos in which it takes place. Everyone voted on most issues related to school affairs, and staff made decisions about bedroom arrangements, finance, and staffing. Over the years they developed a code of written rules, which could, in turn, be changed by vote. This system continues to work to this day (2018) at Summerhill.

Conflict Resolution

We considered developing a similar structure at the Fifteenth Street School, but the young age of the students and the different concerns we had from those of a boarding school made us hesitate. Though the children generally worked and played in an orderly fashion, they also experienced disagreements, anger, hurt feelings, and, at times, both students and teachers lost their tempers. There were the usual children's slights and insults and disputes over equipment, territory, and who could participate in games. Often the kids stated, "It's not fair." Often they found ways to resolve problems on their own. When individuals were involved in a dispute, we spoke with them (in private, when possible) to work out a compromise or stepped in when we felt help was needed.

The discussion might have sounded like this:

Teacher: "Okay, Danny, Darby, what happened"?

Darby: "Danny is always pushing me when I get on the parallel bars."

Danny: "No, I don't, you're the one who won't let me play there."

Darby: "Oh no? Yesterday you tried to pull my leg."

Danny: "Your leg, your leg—you kicked me."

The story could end there, as just the telling and being listened to could yield a solution, or I might say:

"Can you two agree to share the bars?"

"Yeah, just don't pull my leg again."

"Okay, Okay."

I remember how charming, blue-eyed Harry attracted attention on a trip by sidling up to someone, surreptitiously delivering a light jab with his lunchbox and melting away. A chorus of complaints arose, and we asked Harry to walk next to Wilbur, which he did willingly.

Back in school, I asked Harry for a private talk:

"Harry, you know, on the trip you were hitting people with your lunchbox."

"No, I didn't."

"Harry, several people said that you hit them."

"OK, OK. I'm just doing it for fun."

"You know it hurts when you do that."

"Yes, but I still want to do it."

"Well, if you can do this to the kids then it means that they can do things like that to you."

"I won't let them."

"Then, there'll be fights all the time. That's why we need rules, like you can't hurt anyone, and they can't hurt you, and you don't have to worry, and you can have fun doing things you like." (Kant's categorical imperative goes to school!)

I don't recall how Harry responded or if he ever hit anyone with his lunchbox again, but he had a lot of good times building with blocks, creating dramatic space-exploration scenarios, tending the guinea pigs, and playing in the gym. After school, Wilbur and I discussed the cases and the dynamics behind them. What made Harry behave this way, and how could school be of help?

When disagreements arose about taking roles in dramatic play scenarios, a teacher might suggest making adjustments to the roles: being the big sister instead of the mother, or becoming the ticket taker instead of the conductor, or taking turns doing so. At times, children did this on their own.

We talked with the group to identify areas of conflict, such as insuring that study groups have quiet times and places to work and concentrate while others wanted to have active play at the same time. In this case, the teachers stated that anyone coming in and disturbing a study group would be asked to go to another part of the school. In practice, though, some children insisted they had the right to enter into any activity at any time. Sometimes they refused to leave, but in the end, the teachers' and peer pressure prevailed. The child would go to the gym and let off steam or find refuge in the secretary's office, where Margaret and her Chihuahua could always be counted on to lend a friendly ear in a hospitable setting. In that sense, no one was punished but had to respect the needs of others.

At times, we called the group together for discussions to arrive at a consensus for rules, such as setting a reasonable time limit on using the gym bars and other school equipment. The children accepted the underlying logic in the process, and together we tried to be attentive to the individuals' concerns. The difficult part of resolving conflicts lay in the fact that one might have to give up something to arrive at a fair solution. Children might solve problems in unexpected ways, as when someone had an insight into the fact that a fellow student was especially needy of having more cars than his share for his construction or more time with the guitar. There were disappointments, and the process of negotiating and compromising was not always smooth and stretched out over time.

Talks with individuals or a group certainly did not solve every problem or prevent acting-out behavior, but it set a forum for venting, being heard, and weighing options. Though we did not keep written records about problem-solving activities, the accumulation of these events formed a body of precedents, a common history we could call on. Each step set the framework from which to negotiate future disagreements. These methods of dealing with problems set the children's minds at ease, knowing there was adult protection and a rational social order where solutions were sought in a non-punitive atmosphere.

Reflections on Problem Solving

Wilbur wrote about discipline:
◄ The test of discipline as contrasted with the imposition of adult authority is whether the children reasonably manage their affairs when not directly supervised by adults. No doubt conflicts and difficulties will arise and adults will be called upon in any situation, but in those that support self-regulation, the children will be less reactive and more self-disciplined. They *were* at the school. And this means, again, that they had more ownership of their own lives in school than children ordinarily do. From this context comes a great deal of well-being.

We had a relative scarcity of "discipline problems." On the whole, there was such a good feeling about being in the school that most problems were relatively easy to deal with. The most remarkable difference between the Fifteenth Street School and the usual school was the fact that the teacher need not be in the room for reasonable behavior of children to continue. People who visited the school were often amazed to see the children involved in activities without adult supervision. In many schools, all hell breaks loose when a teacher leaves the room. ►

Because most of the children found life in school interesting, they looked forward to being there. They missed attending when we closed for holidays and were puzzled why students they met on the bus from other schools couldn't wait for vacations.

The atmosphere of openness facilitated a sense of easy communication and above-board behavior. We were able to work on problems as they occurred, and most did not fester and develop into resentment. It was an ongoing process, with the ups and downs of human interaction, and everyone had to be constantly involved and thinking about ways and structures for coping with their needs and feelings.

From their idea of justice as "being fair" to understanding that this applied not just to their own concerns, the children developed a social contract. As they gradually internalized the concept, they were able to create their Problem-Solving Committee (discussed later in the Social Studies section).

This is not to say that no social or behavioral problems existed, and there were types of behavior for which we could find no resolution. A few children, most admitted from other schools, did not relate to the school program or to children or adults. They tended to wander around, looking bored, and did not respond to our attempts to interest them in activities. We had to accept that we were not able to meet their needs and, by mutual agreement with their parents, they left the school. In spite of these limitations, I still believe that the relatively low incidence of conflict at the Fifteenth Street School was due to an underlying trust and good faith, a spirit of affection, and camaraderie we all shared.

Voices of Children

Humor and Playfulness

Wilbur and Orson's witty personalities and high spirits created an atmosphere of delight and levity in the school. Sometimes teachers and children alike used humor to defuse tense situations.

The children felt encouraged to create their comic shows with parodies of TV programs and commercials, as well as weather and news commentators. They relished puns and play on words, and Billy coined the often-repeated phrase: "This is an order from General Custard!"

Wilbur wrote about the value of humor:

◄ Children are given to seriousness and playfulness. It is their nature to be serious in their striving to know the world fully and become competent in the behavioral values of society. Both qualities are basic, essential components of the living organism; both are expressive of the vitality of life.

The source of gaiety, the humor, wit, joy and laughter of children derives from the rhythm of life itself, from the expression of high spirits. The open, the free spirit responds to and expresses humor with a sense of exhilaration and pleasure, and humor brings the exuberance of life to the fore.

Dour commentators may interpret the use of humor as causing "a feeling of superiority," but another mechanism is also at work, one that establishes community, a rejoicing in a shared humanity.

At our school we sometimes used humor in a good-natured "topsy-turvy" kind of way, to point out the absurdity of a situation by positing the opposite of what was intended. I might say, "Kids, don't think that school is a place for fun, so get serious and wipe those smiles off your faces," followed by: "How dare you! You disobedient child!! Wipe that smile off your face immediately! If you continue, you'll be punished: we are going to cook popcorn later, and you'll be forced to eat it!!" ►

Voices of Children

Wilbur continues:

◄ Consider the play fights with foam balls held in the gym. A topsy-turvy for sure: vigorous, assertive, aggressive action, cries of warning, delight, pretended wounds.

"Help me! I'm done for," as the child flops to the floor and writhes about.

In these situations, the gloom is dispelled, and humor is a means of expressing the way it is, acknowledging foibles. The child applies it to her/his own behavior, as well as to that of the adult.

Freud has suggested the mechanism involved in some forms of humor, which seems to be applicable to many of our "funny" stories. The formulation which most concerns us is that of humor that comes from the pleasure of experiencing our present mastery over what was formerly painful or difficult. Thus one of the most obvious sources of humor for children, as well as adults, is contained in the free manipulation of language in such a way that one becomes a master of it. ►

At times, children adopted Wilbur's topsy-turvy spirit, as exemplified in the note Allan slipped under Wilbur's door.

Aside from our conversations, we found examples of word play and humorous, imaginative rhymes and stories in the writings of Lewis Carroll, Edmund Lear, William Steig, as well as folk tales. Using humor, wit, drollness, and absurdity created space for a textured, nuanced view of life and encouraged inventiveness in confronting the unexpected.

Social Interaction

Every school has its particular kind of social atmosphere. At the Fifteenth Street School, children engaged in the usual types of personal associations: having a best friend, forming and reforming little groups, with some children feeling excluded and having disputes over ownership and insults. Yet a sense of mutual respect dominated the atmosphere.

The School in Action

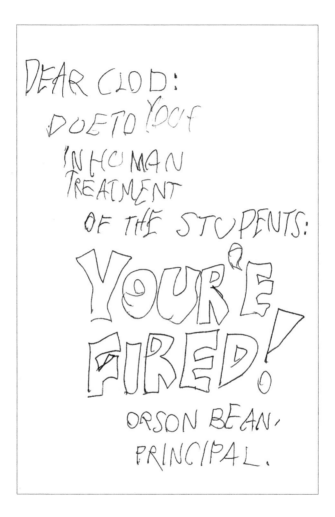

Allan's note.

Voices of Children

Foam fight in the gym.

The children in each age group were involved in their own activities, and being on different floors, did not mix often. The four- and five-year-olds stayed primarily in their classroom on the second floor and sometimes wandered up or down. The older kids enjoyed visiting the younger group, whom they affectionately referred to as "the little kids." In the gym, as well, the groups mixed but played primarily with their classmates.

Girls and boys mixed freely and treated each other as equals. They felt equally free to express emotions, such as sadness and anger.

Wilbur wrote about gender:

◄ We want all children to be self-reliant and assertive, but we noted differences of nuance, tenor and tone between boys and girls. ►

In the gym, boys and girls joined together in acrobatics, dramatic play, and active games such as foam fights and freeze tag. They participated in creating shows and constructs, such as Troll City (discussed in the Social Studies section), and all enjoyed attending cooking and sewing sessions. At the same time, they were influenced by subtle cultural influences about roles, and we observed differences in their choice of activities. Boys were more frequently involved in block building, space-, army-, and dinosaur-related activities, while girls tended to work with art materials, congregate in groups to chat, and engage in dramatic play with dress-up clothes. Girls and boys formed their separate bands and singing groups but performed for everyone.

While being aware of the differences in the children's attitudes, we hoped to foster widespread participation by boys and girls in all activities. Though, at that time of social change, with strong women and sensitive men in the public and private arenas, the concept of gender equality was just emerging in the popular consciousness. I believe that in today's climate of wider acceptance, we would find more ways to encourage everyone to find expression in a broader range of non-stereotypical roles.

Playing a game.

School Ethos

Wilbur recounts an event in the gym that exemplifies the tone of the relationships that prevailed in the school:

◄ One morning in our second year, I walked into the gym where the kids were engaged in rough-and-tumble play on the mats or racing around in a game of freeze tag. Moving to the side, I sat down and called to them to join me for a moment. They came over and sat down in a circle on the floor. I was ready to make an announcement about the visitors who were soon to arrive, when I noticed a bemused expression on their faces. Terry, a recent recruit, age seven, continued to race around the gym, motioning to the children to join him.

"Ummmm!" I thought, "So now we will have first-hand experience regarding his recent expulsion from his last school."

I called on him to join us. He hesitated, took another turn, and with a scowl came to sit with us. It was apparent that the children, by virtue of their experience, had come to the conclusion that I most likely had something to say, or else I would not interrupt their play. Further, they regarded Terry's behavior as passing strange. Some continued to look at him with an air of curiosity, but otherwise the event went unnoticed, and I proceeded with the announcement.

"Today, we'll have visitors, two or three, who want to know more about the school. Nothing unusual about that, except that they will spend the entire day with us."

Gloria, always quick to ferret out the undisclosed agenda, asked, "What do they want?"

"They are from the Department of Education. They visit all newly opened schools to make certain..."

I paused, searching for the right phrase, "That things are going well."

Again Gloria, out of the mouths of babes, "What do you want us to do?"

"Well, aren't things going well?"

A chorus of "Yeah." "Yes, sure." "I love this school." "It's the greatest!"

Voices of Children

Wise, oh, wise Gloria.

"Yeah, but on the school bus, the other kids" (meaning children going to other schools in the neighborhood), "say that we don't do anything but play."

Much indignation. But I nevertheless feel obliged to press the issue.

"Well, is that all you do?"

A chorus of "No's." And citations of group study in reading and arithmetic.

"Well, then, go about your business like you always do, and everything will be fine."

"Yeah, but what if Jimmy runs around the gym, saying 'peniwacker' or some of those other words. You know what I mean."

"I know. I also know that they have heard those words before. Look, we aren't into faking it. Just act like your usual nutty selves, and we'll be fine."

They did. The inspectors did their veni, vidi, and we conquered. We, the teachers and administrators, were pleased, not only about receiving certification, but also about the kids' support of the school. Whether Jimmy said any of "those words," I neither knew nor cared… ➤

By interrupting their play and responding to Wilbur's call, the children demonstrated their regard for their teacher as a rational authority, one who represented the broader world and its demands and at the same time respected their interests and needs. As Neill would say, "He was on their side," and he could be trusted to use his power to protect their well-being.

The new student, Terry, acting in an automatic challenge response, gradually realized that his behavior was out of synch with the other children's, and he was moved to join the group. In this way, the ethos, the school culture, influenced his behavior, interestingly enough without any words being exchanged.

Also of note in this exchange, is the dialogue between teacher and students and the forthright discussion that took place. The children demonstrated their interest and curiosity in the business of their school and their desire to participate in facing the problems that the

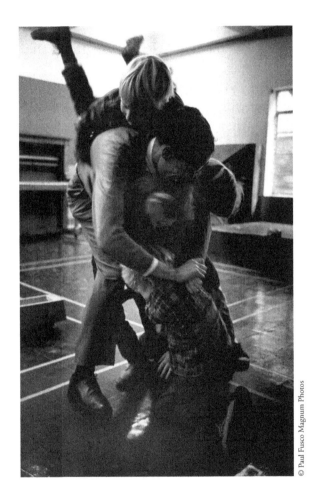

Fun in the gym.

Voices of Children

inspection might present. In telling the kids to be "their usual nutty selves," Wilbur was signaling that the demands of the world (inspection) could and would be coped with in a straightforward way, and that who they were and what they were doing in school had recognized value in the outside world.

At the same time, I am pleased to report that the children did not always respond immediately to requests by the teachers. I recall a time when I sat around a table with four girls and tried to tell them about a trip we were going to take. They were not in the mood to listen and interrupted with unrelated comments and loud laughs.

"Quiet down now so I can finish talking," I told them.

More of the same. At last, I lost it with, "Okay now, the next person who shouts out will have to leave the room. Who is it going to be?"

Without losing a beat, Kim replied, "We don't know yet!"

"Look! This is a Real City!"

Wilbur wrote about a child's observation:

◄ In one corner, near the window, a child is lying on a blanket reading a book. Another looks up from the table where she has been working on a filing system for the class library and says: "This is like a city. Over here is a library, over there the newspaper. Rachel is sewing with the kids and Laura and Darby are painting. Look! This is a real city!" ►

While conventional schools have been compared to factories that Lewis Mumford called the "mega-time machines of society" in which each unit (child or adult) is reduced to a replaceable part, the child's metaphor of the city for school conjures a radically different setting. Of course, we were gratified to hear this analogy for what we were hoping to achieve: a democratic environment where citizens are free to partake in and create an array of meaningful activities in a safe atmosphere. In an ideal city, its citizens can stroll through streets and parks, work and eat, attend lectures, concerts and classes, read quietly in the library, and interact with a variety of people.

The School in Action

At our school, the children explored a variety of settings and face-to-face contacts both inside and outside the building. Inside, they roamed, imagined, built, and created in an extensive domain of rooms, people, animals, books, and materials. They could go from room to room, visit friends, ask questions, interact informally with others, and form their own groups, as well as work independently or attend the organized activities. The children connected with a variety of personalities: their teachers and student teachers, volunteers, Margaret the secretary, and her dogs, as well as Orson and Ralph, the young man who came to clean and talked about sports and his travels.

Outside, they met with Hi and Mel in their luncheonette, the workers in Butler's Lumber Yard, and with shopkeepers, dockworkers, and firemen on our neighborhood walks and trips around the city. All these provided models of people at work and offered insights into how they approached their daily tasks. The children were not only studying people doing their jobs, they were involved with them in a mutual exchange of ideas. While gaining respect for others, their self-esteem was enhanced by seeing themselves as contributors to this extended school community to which they belonged.

Wilbur reflected:

◄ This feeling of life involvement, of relatedness, is what counts. The activities were not there to entertain the children or to seduce them into learning. They were there because the children were interested and became involved in the skills and work functions of the society, because they met the children's need for rational expression of their dynamic drive toward competency and growth. ►

In order to be free, people in a city need to feel safe and protected by rules for traffic and codes for building and conduct. The school met health, safety and certification requirements, but we had no written documents pertaining to conduct. Unlike Summerhill and Sudbury Valley Schools, where the self-governing bodies had developed written codes for regulating and enforcing the social contract, we did not. We spoke about rules at various times and relied on shared assumptions, consensus and discussions. Over time, we developed concepts for guiding behavior that everyone agreed on, and the children created their own guides. (See chapter 5: Social Studies).

Voices of Children

Museum of baby dinosaurs.

The School in Action

And just as in a city the public participates in creating its libraries, theaters, newspapers and rules of behavior, the children took part in creating the school. They developed their presses and publications, library, museums, music and drama groups, TV and radio stations.

The Fifteenth Street School constituted a network for facilitating formal and informal learning. It was a lively environment, where children made decisions about their pursuits, expanded their social skills, and acquired self-discipline in making choices. Yes, in many respects, the school was "a real city" for living and learning.

Listening to the Beatles.

Voices of Children

Goals of the School

Of the primary goals, none was more important to our effort than the other.

For teachers

To develop initiative in exploration of learning activities, with the children feeling pleasure in ownership of their lives and in actual learning, doing, skill-building.

At the level of the primary school, to teach skills of communication in such ways that the child associates books, reading, and writing with the satisfaction of mastery.

For children

To experience delight in feelings of competency, confidence, independent thinking, liveliness, and alertness, and to maintain spiritedness, yes, even gaiety, within the learning process.

To retain a sense of wonder and curiosity and develop a love of beauty and creativity.

To *expand* one's knowledge of the world and develop respect for its inhabitants and laws.

To achieve individuality in the choice of activity — not everyone doing the same thing — while being able to work in a group.

For teachers and children

To maintain an attitude of convivial openness between child and teacher in a community practicing democratic values.

Supporting Self-Directed Learning

The following chapters deal with the content areas we introduced for study, and how teachers and students interacted in the process of learning and teaching. Since Wilbur and I kept records of our activities, I am able to describe highlights of our program and the effects we observed. Here are some of the theories on which we based those experiences.

Many researchers and educators have studied child behavior to decipher the operation of the underlying mental structures that select and convert information into significant knowledge that enables one to function in the world.

Wilbur wrote about how children learn:

◄ "Self-Regulation" is the term used by A.S. Neill to describe the biological means by which the body maintains a rational presence in the world. Basically, it is the capacity to engage in the rational behavior that maintains a process of well-being, serving both the psyche and soma, and the interactive process between the two. It means the rational regulation of the self and the internal dynamic of character development. The body regulates its basic functions, such as breathing, eating, eliminating, sleeping, and organ functions by a process of *homeostasis*. That the process can become unbalanced by the irrational is apparent.

Self-Regulation is evident in the learning process in which children engage in self-initiated activities, such as observation, inquiry, testing, internalizing, and transforming information.

Consider the multiple tasks the infant so willingly, so strenuously undertakes in its first three years of life. In learning to walk, from the first tentative movements to the initial crawling and toddling, the upsy-daisies, the falling down and going boom, the child tenaciously returns to the self-imposed task with confidence and delight. The child's celebration is in the move from surprise and at times outrage at the unwanted upsy-daisy, to the incorporation of frailty as a source of pleasure and gaiety.

"Fall down and go boom" is played out in a victory enactment. In "London Bridge Is Falling Down" and "Little Sally Walker" we celebrate our hard-earned victory over gravity not by outlandish fireworks, but by making the fall a primary metaphor of speech. The event is acknowledged through the ritual of song and movement.

Parallel experiences accompany the process of learning to eat with utensils, learning the benefits of the bathroom, and above all learning to speak in the steady process of one-word utterances on to the structured grammar of sentences and statements.

In *Language in the Crib*, Ruth Hirsch Weir writes, "Nowhere is the self-regulated learning process more evident than in the acquisition of language."

While it is evident that the adult's supportive, interactive role is hardly insignificant, the accomplishments would not be fully realized if they did not derive from the infant's inner resources (often attributed to automatic motivation), not alone the initiative taken in learning, but the pleasure in doing so.

The emphasis here is on the child's undertakings and the adult's significance as role model and direct intervention in the games of the child's infancy, such as "Peek-a-Boo," "Where, Oh Where Did Little Susie Go?" and "This Little Piggy."

The interaction, the shared pleasure, the satisfaction offered by skills attained, by knowledge accrued, and by sharing between child and adult are basic to the responsive learning environment and integral to its processes.

Before reaching school age, children have learned a variety of skills for coping with day-to-day activities. The child moves from pointing randomly, to pointing to objects he/she desires, to being able to obtain such objects sometimes by making this known to others. Thus, through a series of actions and reactions children have become involved in a

The School in Action

process of making deductions, comprehending, memorizing, adapting, and incorporating structures needed for functioning in the world. ➤

From their observations of children at play, and in controlled learning situations, child behavior researchers theorized about ways children process information and ideas.

Jean Piaget and Lev Vygotsky developed theories about the universal patterns of children's thought processes and their stages of maturation.

Jean Piaget investigated "cognitive processes" and described the stages of maturation through which abilities to absorb and integrate information develops. Jerome Bruner described cognitive processes as "the means whereby organisms achieve, retain and transform information."

Lev Vygotsky's concept of "constructivist learning" asserts that learning takes place in social exchanges involving dialogue. He observed and wrote about the sequence in which learning takes place. It begins with a gradually developing awareness of new thoughts from which new learning emerges. Vygotsky calls this stage the "proximal zone."

The zone of proximal development defines those functions that have not matured, but are in the process of maturation, functions that will mature but are currently in an embryonic state. According to Vygotsky, these functions could be termed "buds or flowers" of development rather that the "fruits" of development.

By being aware of the stage of readiness that precedes the time of extending one's knowledge, educators can enhance the conditions for its unfolding. Today, research in brain development corroborates most of the findings of these and other researchers. Many of these concepts about learning were in our minds as we proceeded to set up our program for learning and teaching.

Howard Gardner developed the concept of "multiple intelligences" and describes the various faculties through which learning is processed: In *The Theory of Multiple Intelligences*, he argues that there is "… persuasive evidence for the existence of several relatively autonomous human intellectual competencies," which he calls "frames of mind."

Wilbur's thoughts:

◄ Intelligence is therefore not a single mindset but manifests itself in a variety of separate modes such as: musical, linguistic, spatial, bodily/kinesthetic, and inter/intra personal. The implications are many. The much relied-on I.Q. tests, for instance, measure intelligence of a particular kind and show nothing about a variety of other competencies the person tested may hold. The tests, according to Gardner, have predictive power for success in schooling, but relatively little predictive power outside the school context. ►

As our culture places greatest value on verbal/linguistic and logical/mathematical intelligence, other modes of intelligence, which may predominate in individuals and consist of valuable avenues for learning, are often overlooked. Though we intuitively recognized their existence, at our school we did not have a schematized program for addressing and evaluating them.

Wilbur wrote about his observations of children's interactions with the world and about the ideas that influenced our thinking:

◄ All things are subject to change. Nothing is fixed or permanent. This includes the living as well as the phenomenological world of the elements, the sky, oceans and continents, the moon, sun, the planets and stars above, and the so-called inert natural things, such as the very earth we walk on, sand, water, air, and mud.

Children are subject to multitudinous transformations originating from their bodies: growing from baby to the present, the process of eating and digestion, going from babble to speech. They observe changes as parents and family members come and go, day turns into night, and weather and the seasons bring hot and cold temperatures. They see water freezing and melting, turning into rain and snow, and eggs developing into tadpoles, caterpillars into butterflies, seeds into plants, leaves growing and falling, birth and death.

The School in Action

Given the incessant shifts in their world, their versatility in maintaining themselves intact seems miraculous. By using their imagination – a particular play of intelligence – children are able to command and exert power over the raw materials of the world. They experience themselves as active agents when they observe and understand the nature of objects and events and can use their creativity to transform materials and ideas into their own images and concepts. They need to be engaged in the world and feel reassured that, in some part, they can deal with its mystery and fashion it themselves.

A child splashing around in a puddle to control the movement of the water contrasts with that which we have no power to affect, that which comes without warning and overwhelms us with its propulsion, wars, loss, natural disasters. When children have no control, they perceive things as arbitrarily coming and going, appearing and disappearing without explanation.

With their active imaginations, children are creatures given to reinvention; nothing is so lowly as to escape their attention.

"What can you do with it?" is the first question they ask when appraising an object.

Tin cans and a board: Voilà! A vehicle!

Sand: A castle.

A blade of grass, a flattened bottle top bent in half, pierced with a hole: A whistle.

When is a guinea pig not a guinea pig? When it's an astronaut or a politician.

When is a stick not a stick? When it's a conductor's baton, a sword, or a noisemaker to rattle along fences, an extension to stir up muddy puddles, the occasion to be told: "Watch it! You're gonna poke someone's eye out if you don't be careful!"

Verbal maneuvers are critical as children seek empowerment, and the voice with its multiple variations, offers the greatest of all possibilities. The infant and the young child play with sound, rhyme, humor, later creating stories, fantasies.

Children's lives are replete with instances of self-initiated, self-regulatory development, and adults can contribute by eliciting responses that will engage children in relating to their world. ➤

Here are descriptions of some of the ways in which the children experienced the learning process at the Fifteenth Street School.

Though the topics we studied are listed in discreet categories, they frequently merged into integrated units. For instance: the children's *Farm of the Six* (as we discuss later) began with studying plants and their environments and ended in considering issues of governance, ecology, and ethics.

This process is in line with Gestalt and Social Constructivist learning theories indicating that learning takes place in a social context, with the grasping of wholes as opposed to atomized, dissociated units. Current studies of brain development corroborate these theories.

Learners Collaborate

The areas we covered: language and math skills, the arts, science, and social studies were not unique to the Fifteenth Street School and approximated the curricula of progressive and public schools. What was unique was the collaboration of students and teachers in making choices and the informal style of proceeding without preset time frames. Our goal was to introduce relevant study material, as well as to follow the students' ideas, and encourage them to react with their individual responses and creative faculties. We planned and reflected on the activities that originated from the ongoing dialogue between teachers and students.

We also consulted various study guides, including those from the New York City Board of Education. In addition to our offerings, friends of the school and some parents skilled in sewing, origami, gymnastics, and cooking volunteered to work with groups.

The School in Action

Cooking pea soup.

Wilbur recalled a particular example:

◄ Mrs. Schwartz (a parent) came once a week and worked with small rotating groups of eager cooking students. The recipes were written out on easel-sized paper and were posted for reading practice. ►

One of the graduates reminisced:

We made great stuff from scratch: pineapple upside-down cake and gingerbread houses, noodles in as many shapes as we could come up with, and tomato sauce to go with the abstract pasta forms.

Sing-ins, holiday gatherings, children's skits, and school meetings took place in the gym, where everyone looked forward to Orson's wonderful magic shows.

Children pursued group activities, as well as their individual interests such as reading, drawing, painting, constructing, talking with friends and teachers, playing with animals, physical activity, or musing. They made choices from the array of available activities, and we would announce a time for science, art, and music activities or special events. Those that were interested gathered to participate, and the school was small enough that everyone could be apprised and plan to attend.

Children had their individual ways of relating to the group,, and all seemed to have a virtual map of the rooms and their place in it. Everyone accepted that some kids had their own spaces where they drew or read. Others kept a distance, monitoring the group till they felt safe to join.

In the following chapters, I describe how the curriculum developed over the four years we worked at the Fifteenth Street School. I write about the topics and themes that emerged, rather than in the chronological order in which events occurred.

Art is the uniting of the subjective with the objective,
of nature with reason, of the unconscious with the conscious,
and therefore art is the highest means of knowledge.

– Leo Tolstoy

Chapter 3

The Arts: A Child's First Language

Every culture has a form of art, and, before they can communicate with words, children everywhere generate their own art. Art is the first language through which they express themselves, as well as the symbol system for interpreting and constructing knowledge and the meaning of their world. Playing with objects, children create visual forms and songs and dances with sounds and movements.

As McArdle, Felicity and Wright, and Susan Kay wrote in 2014 in *Literacy in the Arts*, "Young children can be expressing astonishing conceptual understanding and imagination well beyond what they can communicate through language."

Creating Our Visual Arts Program

As children develop their physical, visual, and verbal abilities, they add narratives to their creative expressions and enter the stage for learning linguistic and numerical symbol systems. Continuous practice in the arts supports children's physical, emotional, and social development and expands the brain's capacity to learn and master the symbol systems and skills children need to function in the world. One of our goals at the Fifteenth Street School was to provide materials and opportunities for the children's creative expression, and the arts pervaded most of the activities.

Over our years of teaching, Wilbur and I watched with wonder as young children spontaneously explored and experimented with the textures, shapes, and colors of paper, clay, sand, wood, and whatever other materials they could find. Children draw and paint with fingers, and later on, with crayons, pencils, and brushes. Their artistic growth generally follows the developmental stages that Viktor

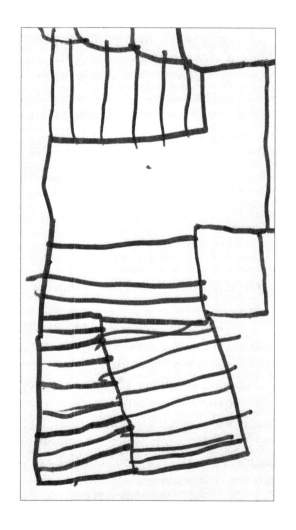

Voices of Children

Lowenfeld observed in his extensive research. Children begin by spontaneously drawing lines, then shapes, and figure out ways to combine shapes and lines to represent figures and scenes. Over time, the children refine and elaborate their imagery. Lowenfeld found this growth pattern to be self-generated and universal.

At our school, we set up the art room to resemble an artist's studio, where children accessed materials to create their own images. The children worked independently or in groups, and our beginning six-year-old group had entered what Lowenfeld called the "schematic stage." They combined lines and shapes to create images as well as picture stories. As not everyone develops at the same pace, there was a wide span in the children's abilities to articulate the subjects they wished to portray.

The art room was a popular place where children were able to practice their skills and develop at their own pace. I spent most of my time there, organizing materials and activities as well as group projects such as puppet making, weaving, or mural painting.

Sensory Logic

Using open-ended materials such as unit building blocks, wood, tools, clay, paint, and found objects, the children developed their own ideas and images. They created and recreated objects and structures from their environment and inhabited them through their imaginations. At the same time, these activities strengthened their understanding of the real world.

Boys and girls were equally involved in art activities; girls were more interested in painting and sewing projects such as making dolls and weaving. Boys especially liked to work on three-dimensional objects and decorate their wood and clay creations with paint and found objects like corks or bottle tops. Most everyone felt confident to participate in some form of art making.

The children took pleasure in the doing while gaining competence in developing their skills. Creating signs and stories for their constructions helped with learning reading and writing. They improved

Stitched figures.

their computing skills by measuring and estimating with blocks and wood. They developed physical coordination while mastering the use of tools. Their social skills grew as they cooperated to work on their projects. Without being aware of it, they were learning concepts of math, engineering, architecture, research, and planning. The rooms were filled with the sounds and expressions of vital energy one senses in situations where children are actively engaged in their lives and work. The teachers assisted by observing and encouraging with suggestions, questions, descriptive comments, and technical assistance.

The art educator Judith Burton called this process "sensory logic," the capacity to exert physical actions upon material from which symbols and complex thought would emerge over time.

Topics and Media

Using paper, paint, pens, pencils, crayons, and magic markers, the children created images from the world around them, as well as fantasy monsters and super-heroes from their imagination. They also drew cartoons and illustrations for stories, social studies subjects, and the school newspaper, *The Squeaker Times*.

When the children began drawing portraits of each other and people they knew, I suggested they could model and draw pictures of their classmates. Several children met regularly to pose and draw and talk about their work. The students also depicted events relating to our trips around the city. When we studied American history, they depicted scenes and made models of Native American and Inuit life. As part of our "cold" model, we hung a poster of U.S. presidents that inspired the children to paint portraits of their favorites, often Washington and Lincoln.

The children used some of their artwork in books they made, and some we displayed on walls or bulletin boards for all to see. These art activities were ongoing, and in the social context of the school, most everyone connected and reacted to each other's works. I assisted them by suggesting topics, reflecting, and answering questions.

The Arts: A Child's First Language

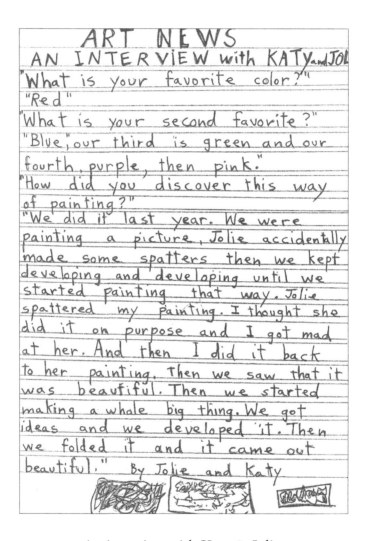

ART NEWS
AN INTERVIEW with KATY and JOL

"What is your favorite color?"

"Red"

"What is your second favorite?"

"Blue, our third is green and our fourth, purple, then pink."

"How did you discover this way of painting?"

"We did it last year. We were painting a picture, Jolie accidentally made some spatters then we kept developing and developing until we started painting that way. Jolie spattered my painting. I thought she did it on purpose and I got mad at her. And then I did it back to her painting. Then we saw that it was beautiful. Then we started making a whole big thing. We got ideas and we developed it. Then we folded it and it came out beautiful." By Jolie and Katy

An interview with Katy & Jolie.

Voices of Children

Experimenting with Color

The children worked at a table with containers of primary colors and black-and-white tempera paint set on a metal tray that the children used as a palette. They mixed colors on the tray with a single brush and could mix new colors after cleaning the brush by dipping it into a cup of water and dabbing it on a sponge. They also painted at an easel set up with paint in cups.

Gradually, the children learned to mix predictable formulas by combining primary colors and adding black and white to produce tints and shades. With this knowledge, they could plan for specific images: a purple dress, green leaves, or brown hair.

They often shared what they were discovering with their fellow painters: "Hey! Red and yellow makes orange." "What will happen if you add white or black?" I might ask. When Jolie and Katy wanted to talk about their paintings, I recorded the interview (left), which was published in the Art News section of *The Squeaker Times*.

Enjoying their playful interaction as they painted, Jolie and Katy became aware that they were engaged in a process of discovery "we kept developing and developing." As they reflected and expressed their thoughts, they realized they had the power to generate new ideas and give them form. ".... then we saw that [our painting] was beautiful. We got ideas and we developed it." They knew that they could intentionally repeat and refine their process of discovery. They learned from their play. They learned from each other. Sharing their insights about their newly found powers was an important part of their experience. The art educators Edith Gwathmey and Ann Marie Mott (2014) have observed and written about the import of children's exchanges relating to their art-making:

"[At the art table] children were continually looking at each other's artwork, asking questions and making comments about their own or their friends' paintings. As they worked… they were exchanging and communicating ideas in both verbal and non-verbal domains. Their visual perceptual behaviors, physical gestures and verbalizations to themselves, to each other, and to their teachers seemed to bounce back and forth around the large table."

Voices of Children

I have observed this behavior in all school populations where teachers support and encourage children's expressions.

At the Fifteenth Street School, some children liked to mix for a long time until the colors turned gray or brown. They manipulated the viscous nature of paint and covered sheets of paper with their mixtures. Over these, they dripped more colors in the style of Jackson Pollock. They were excited as they observed and hypothesized about their unfolding creations.

This is the kind of conversation I would hear in the art room:

"I wonder how blue is going to look in it. Look, it's getting darker."

"Wow! Mine looks like mountains."

"Yeah! How did you do it?"

The children created abstract forms in which they discerned color and surface variations: shapes rising like mountains or ocean waves, flat and winding like lakes, rivers, and roads. They saw gradations from light to dark, homes of monsters or super-heroes, and whales and dolphins rising from the depths. They also drew and painted abstract shapes, sometimes using simple lines of various widths on a page in the style of Franz Kline.

The children called their mixtures "color experiments" and these were similar to the science experiments they were conducting in their Kitchen Science lab down the hall. In the art room, someone tried another experiment by pressing a blank sheet of paper over a painting. Voila! A mirror image: a mono-print. This reminded me of a boy I observed in an "inner city" public school where I once taught. He discovered how to make mono-prints by pressing brown paper towels, which I brought from the bathroom, over his paintings. At our school, other children followed suit and made their own mono-prints. We showed them how to make prints from plants, objects, carved erasers, and eventually linoleum cuts. We also produced mechanical prints on the mimeograph machine.

Are these types of children's experiments art, or are they science? The common denominator is the children's curiosity to explore how various substances and techniques interact, their inspiration to move matter and discover new entities. It's the same drive that propels

Voices of Children

artists and scientists in their quests for knowledge of the world. Of course, eventually, scientific results must be tested rigorously, while the arts rely essentially on intuition and the unique quality of the creative work.

Children share a universal urge to know their world that leads them to ask questions and investigate all areas of experience. They direct their own learning process, and sometimes adults become allies in their search.

Exploring Clay

We kept clay in a metal container, and the children took pleasure in exploring the properties of this plastic material. Clay responds to body movements, and the children pounded, squeezed, pulled, stretched, twisted, and rolled it into balls, pancakes, cubes, and coils. The children combined shapes to create figures and animals: a ball could become a torso; a smaller one a head; and four small coils, arms and legs. They learned how to smooth shapes together and draw on them with tongue depressors, nails, and pencils. They also learned to mold figures, animals, and small pots from lumps of clay. The clay table was always a lively place as children announced their discoveries: "Hey look, this is turning into a snake—arghhh!!!"

They made food like fruits and hamburgers as well as abstract sculptures in the form of spheres, ovoids, and cubic shapes. They placed their creations on a shelf to dry and observed how clay changed from a wet pliable substance to a hard brittle one. As we didn't have a kiln, the children painted and sometimes shellacked their work. Alex painted a chicken leg brown.

"This is a birthday present for my father," he said. "It's his favorite thing."

Story illustration.

Finding and Using Objects

Wilbur and I were eternal collectors of interesting discarded objects and brought back shells, pieces of worn glass and wood, pebbles, leaves, twigs, and grasses from our trips to the beach and country. We also collected stones and leaves with the kids in the park, and parents and friends contributed various objects such as wine corks, buttons, ice cream sticks, yarns, and fabrics.

At Bank Street, Lois Lord had taught us how to classify and organize found objects into shallow containers for easy access, and we sorted and arranged our treasures in boxes and trays. The children learned to cut and fit shapes together from wood, yarns, and cloth and to glue and staple assorted objects. From these collections grew imaginary forests, gardens, animals, people and structures, puppets, and abstract forms.

Lois Lord also taught us to cut paper into squares and rectangles and display them for the children to assemble into figures or abstract forms. They could tear their own shapes and combine them with found objects. They glued these aggregates to pieces of paper or cardboard or made freestanding assemblages. The children also used torn paper for shaping and gluing into paper mache puppets, figures, and animals.

For their space stations, museums, and troll and dinosaur homes, the children cut, shaped, and decorated boxes and made figures from clay and other materials. They created costumes and navigation instruments from various objects, fabrics, and plastics.

Just as we brought recordings to hear the work of musicians, we brought art books to share the works of artists. We talked about how Picasso used his imagination to combine various materials into figures and animals. We looked at the shapes and colors Paul Klee used to make paintings. As they pursued their art making, the children could find echoes of their own images and methods in these works.

Constructing with Wood

In the wood room, boys and girls practiced their building skills. They sawed wood, hammered nails, drilled holes, assembled the pieces, and painted and decorated them with various materials. The children used the cars, planes, figures, and furnishings they made as props for their block buildings and dramatic play.

I now wonder what inspired Wilbur and some kids to build a large wooden structure they called "the bus." Together they hypothesized about its size—how long and wide it needed to be to hold passengers—and estimated how much wood they needed to build it. They made judgments about how to cut and join the wood to fit into a coherent structure. When the bus was ready, they took it to the gym where everyone could "ride" in it and invent scenarios.

"All aboard." called the conductor, handing out tickets to various destinations.

·"Coney Island. Last stop," he announced as the passengers scattered to various parts of the gym.

Children have always engaged in taking imaginary trips with imaginary props and, as in the stories they tell, they are able to "rehearse" life in the broader world without having to deal with the consequences that would occur in real-life situations.

Without introduction, we laid a board and a box of small wood scraps and bottles of glue on a table. Someone glued a few scraps together, and others added their own. For the next weeks anyone who came by could add to this growing sculpture. As each placed her piece of wood she had to figure out how it would balance and fit into the emerging design. Often several people gathered to comment and take turns. When they thought it was complete, the children brought paints to the table for everyone to participate in covering the sculpture with color. This group effort took on a life of its own. When we hung the sculpture in the hall, passers-by took pride in pointing to the sections they or their friends had contributed.

In all these enterprises, the children were the planners, designers, and craftspeople as they collaborated to construct their projects.

Constructing with found objects.

The Arts: A Child's First Language

Though there were occasional disputes about belongings or territory, a general spirit of teamwork prevailed. It seemed the pleasure in creating had its own dynamic.

Building with Blocks and Other Objects

"The smooth shapely maple blocks with which to build, the sense of which never afterward leaves the fingers: so form became feeling," wrote Frank Lloyd Wright about the Froebel blocks he had played with as a boy. Wright felt the blocks were a vital part of his inspiration for his architectural work: "Here was something for invention to seize, and use to create," he noted.

This structural material, invented by Froebel in the mid-nineteenth century, embodied aesthetic and mathematical concepts. Children were attracted to the blocks' forms and textures and enjoyed manipulating them. The blocks were the forerunners of Caroline Pratt's Unit Blocks, Cuisenaire Rods, and Legos.

Wilbur wrote about his first experience with the Pratt Unit Blocks:

◄ "How do people get in and out of this building? Is there a door? And windows? How do people inside get air?" asks a teacher in the block area at the City and Country School.

I first learned about blocks and their remarkable qualities as a student teacher. I also learned how to observe and dialogue with the builders about their constructions and help them sharpen their observational skills.

Caroline Pratt, who founded the City and Country School in 1914, designed the blocks, and the teachers still use them from nursery through sixth grade. The blocks are not only a structural material; they are the core of the school's activities. The smoothly sanded pieces of unpainted maple consist of multiples of square and rectangular shapes measuring 1 3/8" x 2 3/4" x 5 1/2" and include size-correlated cylinders, triangles, arches, and ramps.

Pleasant to the touch, these geometric forms embody a mathematical symbol system. While building with them, chil-

At the workbench.

Working on the bus.

The Arts: A Child's First Language

Block building
of the United Nations.

Voices of Children

dren experience the regularities of the blocks' length, volume, width, and height and also engage in mathematical operations such as addition, subtraction, division, and multiplication.

The children replicate structures they may have seen on a trip to the community, as well as roads, tunnels, high-rise buildings, docking station for boats, and other points of interest. They also build imaginary environments, castles and caves. The sensory awareness they experience in using the blocks forms the basis for conscious understanding of mathematical concepts. ►

Children build without architectural plans and begin by stacking blocks on top of or next to each other and to make simple enclosures. Through trial and error, they gradually grasp how to estimate the ways the various sizes and shapes fit together and to represent the balanced structures they envision.

In the Wood Room at our school, we arranged the blocks and their accessories in two large shelving units. The accessories consist of wooden cars, trucks, and figures of people, animals, firefighters, and other workers designed to complement the blocks. They are free of the history and associations attached to commercial toys owned by individuals and represent common symbols for all to share.

In most schools, children were asked to park toys from home in their lockers. We thought that in keeping with our goal of encouraging children to use their imaginations and exert choices, they should be allowed to use their own toys such as metal cars and trucks, plastic "monsters" and superheroes, stuffed animals and dolls.

We felt conflicted when some children brought toy guns to school. After discussing the issue with the staff, we concluded that the children's interest in violent scenarios would create opportunities to discuss conflict and their fantasies about war. War was then a hot topic, as the onset of the Vietnam War and the protests against it raged here and abroad.

In our group most of the children had attended nursery school and were ready to undertake building complex structures. Working on their own or in fluid groups, they planned and cooperated to carry out their ideas and engineered replicas of houses, bridges, and airports they had seen or imagined. They built a Museum for Guinea

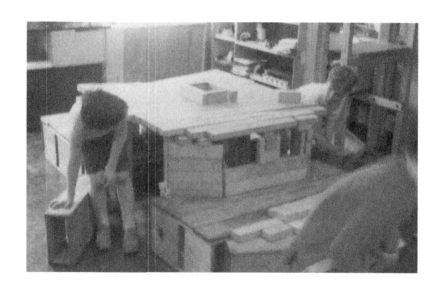

Mixed size block construction.

Pigs, space stations, the George Washington Bridge, as well as abstract designs, castles, and hideaways.

The children expanded their constructions into life-sized structures, and we brought large-scale hollow blocks (approximately one foot square by five inches) and boards to help them realize their ideas. The larger blocks have traditionally been used primarily for outdoor large-muscle play, while the smaller blocks encourage more fine-tuned symbolic representations. We decided to use both and see what the children did with them. They combined all to make body-scaled cars, dwellings, planes, and space vehicles that they "navigated" with instruments made of old machine parts and wood. Moving in and out of these structures, they enacted imaginary scenarios such as space flights and landings, individual journeys in cars and planes, and house play. Vehicles such as the bus and buildings represented the kinds of structures used in our culture that the children wanted to replicate. The projects might last one day or stretch out over weeks, and the teachers were on hand with ideas, technical aid, and resources, such as books, maps, and objects.

Children Create Spaces

Most of us remember the fun we had finding our own private hideaways under a table, in improvised boxes, tents, or caves. In the gym and the upstairs rooms, kids used tables, chairs, shelves, and empty storage drums, covering them with fabrics to create dwellings and hideouts. Inside these, they played dramatic games, ranging from domestic events to battle scenes, and read, chatted, and rested.

Wilbur's thoughts about the process:

◄ The young child, indoors, attempts to build a shelter by placing a blanket over a table or by huddling behind a high chair in the corner of a room. And children are functionalists. If trees are available, of suitable size and kind, near where they live, they will build tree houses. If vacant lots, fields or woods are available, shacks will appear. In the city, children build shacks made of doors and boards whenever demolition

The Arts: A Child's First Language

is going on; in short, whenever adults do not interfere. If no lots or trees are available, children in the city use large cardboard packing cases for the duration that the box survives. ➤

Alas, we rarely see children playing in empty lots these days, as the lots are generally off limits and are quickly covered by large-scale buildings.

Though not everyone built with blocks or created spaces, most children were interested in what their classmates were doing and shared conversations about their activities. I now believe we could have expanded their thinking by setting up sharing times to discuss and record their thoughts about their creations and how they related to the broader world.

Working in the visual arts, children create objects that reflect their ideas and movements, and in the performing arts they primarily express their ideas through their own voices and body movements. At our school, we created opportunities for the children to explore all aspects of the arts.

Making Music

Wilbur used his experiences as a musician to develop music activities with the children. He took pleasure in playing his guitar and singing as the children learned songs and interpreted musical rhythms through their movements.

Singing with the kids, he played "Luby Lu," "Hop Little Squirrel," and "Paw Paw Patch," while the children engaged in their gyrations around the room. He became increasingly versatile in assisting the varieties of their expressions and in providing sound for a range of movement.

Celia and friend, in their hideout.

top & bottom: Improvising and recording songs.

Voices of Children

guinea-pig, magnifying glass, and an Egyptian Mummy. The Museum is open from 12:00 o'clock noon till 9:00 o'clock in the morning. Admission is 2 cents.

Tuesday	NEWS FLASHES	
Anthony is preparing a puppet show called THE CRASHING ROCKS	Louie is adding numbers on a meter	Michele is making a little clay kettle. Lynn is making a little clay cat

DANCE-SHOW IN GYM

On Monday, Margaret, Susie, Darby, Sarah and Laura presented a dance-show in the Gym. Eric was the usher and stage-light man. At intermission, Margaret's birthday was celebrated. Delicious jelly donuts were served and everyone joined together in the dancing.

by Susie and Darby

Dance show in the gym.

Wilbur worked with the children to create and use simple musi-cal instruments. With an old metal tub, he made a washtub bass (aka gutbucket) that the children could strum. They explored sounds by scraping a spoon over an old washboard and learned to make musical instruments from scavenged materials. They cut old curtain rods to size to make rhythm sticks and filled empty film canisters with beans to create maracas; they stretched leather or vinyl over metal cans that became drums and turned metal tops of fiber containers into sounding surfaces. With these, and a set of conventional drums and a guitar, the children formed bands. They created their own music and also accompanied recorded songs.

I am reminded of my teaching in public school and the univer-sality of these experiences. For example, in an after-school program where I had worked, a group of nine-year-old Latino boys, recent arrivals learning English, organized a parade in which they imitated playing drums, flutes, maracas, and guitar as they marched in rhythm to the inaudible music. Their nuanced movements and rapt expressions reflected their grasp of the dynamic of music making and the synchronized workings of a band.

Wilbur also organized a recorder class with conventional instruc-tion and scheduled specific times for these activities. Though we had no formal dance or movement instruction, the children danced to the music of records and organized spontaneous music shows with merry singing and dancing. Everyone enjoyed some form of music activity and could relate to the traditional and contemporary styles that they heard or participated in performing. After improvising a musical show, children talk about how they imagine themselves as grown musicians contemplating their careers.

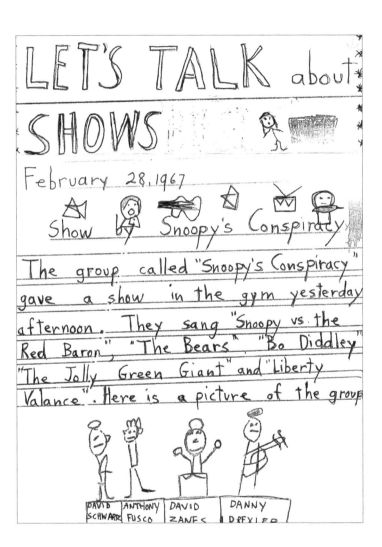

Let's talk about shows.

The Arts: A Child's First Language

🎥 INTERVIEW 🎥

After the show, reporters Louis Offerman and Allan Converse interviewed the members of the group. They asked them how they became singers.

Anthony said "I was watching TV when I was about 19. I saw this great group of 3 or 4 people and I said "That's it I know what my job will be." When I grew up I got a singing group together and called myself Snoopy and my partners Shermi, Charlie Brown and Linus.

After 2 or 3 years of practice the big day finally came we were ready for show business. We called ourselves "Snoopy's Conspiracy"

David Schwarz said "It just came to my mind to be a singer. I use Gleem which made my teeth so white I got in"

Danny Drexler said "I don't know, we just met up together and started singing"

David Zanes "I got the idea from records."

Interview.

Voices of Children

Dramatic Play

The poet Charles Baudelaire wrote in 1853 that "All children talk to their toys; toys become actors in the great drama of life, reduced by the *camera obscura* of their small brains. Children bear witness through their games to their great faculty of abstraction and their high imaginative power."

A century later, Wilbur observed:

◄ Children everywhere engage in spontaneous dramatic play, enacting roles of figures in their environments and imaginations. They reinvent their lives by pretending to be imaginary characters such as storekeepers, truck drivers, firefighters, doctors, nurses, teachers, police officers, and in later years astronauts, soldiers, cowboys, musicians, comedians, actors, dancers, public figures, as well as animals and phantasy figures: witches, monsters, super heroes. They learn to communicate and negotiate with their peers in an imaginary context that serves as a metaphor for the actual world. ►

At our school, the students created spontaneous dramas with their toys and each other. By playing make-believe roles, they re-imagined and projected events in their world: Louis was a radio announcer; Margaret, an acrobat; Allison took turns being a mother, a dog, and a cat; and Billy was an astronaut or NASA operative. They continued these enactments over days until the mothers, fathers, dogs, and pilots decided to end their stories and begin new ones.

The children named some of the themes they created from their dramatic play: The Farm of the Six, Troll City, Space, and Elections. These unfolded over weeks and months, and the children did not intend to repeat them for a performance before an audience.

We teachers helped by affirming the children's imaginary play and supplying props as needed. We brought dress-up clothing for the kids and cardboard boxes for the trolls' apartments. For the Farm of the Six, the children examined fruits and vegetables. On the national scene, Johnson had recently been elected, and we discussed his and Kennedy's personalities and campaign issues to further the children's understanding of their pretend elections of guinea pig and troll candidates.

The Arts: A Child's First Language

Magic marker drawing of dance show.

A Show is Born

Though television was relatively new, by ages six and seven most children had seen live and televised shows. They understood that stories could be scripted and performed before an audience, and at some point they began to create "shows."

I still enjoy thinking about one of the first skits the kids developed: "Lost in Commercials." Returning from a visit to a TV studio, which Orson had arranged, the children talked about commercials they'd seen on their TVs at home. We discussed the fact that commercials were made to sell things and make them sound desirable. Darby drew a picture of a soap carton and improvised a speech that went something like this:

"Super Duper Suds is the purest soap in the world. It takes away small spots and large spots. If you buy Super Duper Suds, your laundry will smell so good everyone will want to be around you."

We all laughed. Clearly, the kids grasped the hyperbolic nature of advertising. Darby's idea spread, and others made posters for toothpaste, aspirin, pizza, and Coca-Cola. They sat around a table, which became their broadcasting studio, and each held up a sign with a product while making pithy comments about the wonders it supposedly produced. At the end, we collected the signs for future use.

"This is like a regular TV show," Anthony remarked. "Let's call it 'Lost in Commercials.'"

The next time we assembled, Anthony headed the meeting and announced: "Ladies and gentlemen, this is Anthony from station WABC bringing you our newest show, 'Lost in Commercials.' First, I will introduce Darby with Super Duper Suds. Thank you."

Wilbur and I were beaming: the children had given birth to an original creation, a complex structure involving thought and discipline. This was the kind of cooperative effort between students and teachers we had envisioned for the school, and it was the start of the children's impromptu theater.

The children repeated "Lost in Commercials" several times with new products and went on to improvise other TV and radio broadcasts. These included weather reports and newscasts based on events in the school and the world, as well as spoofs of actual talk shows and programs they had seen or heard at home.

Wilbur wrote about the development of the children's dramatic activities in the gym:

◄ From the spontaneous, informal play activity of the gym came many dramatic presentations: a rock-and-roll group playing drums, flute and percussion instruments with their own musical renditions; singing and dancing to my guitar playing and to the children's band, as well as to the recorded music of the Beatles and other musicians; a magic show that eight boys and girls made up on their own with props from a set obtained on a birthday; comic shows with sight gags, and circus shows with acrobats, clowns, dancing horses and dancing girls. Some of these were improvised and others planned, scripted and rehearsed.

As the gym lent itself to large muscle activities, some children began to focus their energies on exploring acrobatic moves. They used the large storage drums and monkey bars to support themselves. I provided an additional structure by joining two coat racks together and creating parallel bars. For safety, I placed mats under them.

The children climbed on the bars and swung and hung by their knees, arms and hands. Gradually, the more daring and skilled in motor abilities began to balance themselves on the bars with their feet, walk across them and jump the five-foot height to the mats below.

After a sufficient amount of practice, several children announced that they were going to give an acrobatic show. And so, before their peers and school staff they demonstrated their tricks and feats in an orderly sequence, going from the prosaic knee hangs to daring feats of balancing, all to the background music of the juke box. This show, as simple as it would seem to the observer, was the result of years of development. It started with the first movements of the baby in the crib through crawling, standing upright, walking, climbing, skipping, running and balancing, to the more intensive discipline of practice on the parallel bars day after day. The show was a coherent performance possessing a sense of formal design and drama.

The acrobats received additional support from a friend of the school who taught body movement, and volunteered to help them refine their work and presentations. And as time went on, more children joined the shows. At first the more confident and versatile members of the group had organized and performed in the shows. Yet, gradually students who felt less assured, seeing and feeling a climate of affirmation, gained confidence to participate and make up their own presentations. It proved the adage, 'Nothing succeeds like success.' ►

Planning and Performing Shows

We read the recently published *Improvisation for the Theater* by Viola Spolin (1999) and practiced some of her exercises with the children. These helped them develop their creativity and poise. Any kind of dramatic play requires creating and enacting characters that are representations of oneself or other people, as well as animals and inanimate objects like trains, planes, and cars. In spontaneous dramatic play, a character is expected to maintain a stable interpretation of his role—a baby does not suddenly act like an airplane, or a dog like a human mother. While inventing the stories they act out, children are learning to play by rules that they generally don't articulate unless someone lapses out of a chosen part.

When they were ready to present scripted shows, the children grasped that their scenarios needed to have content to hold their audience's interest. In both their spontaneous and scripted plays they were exercising their memories, imaginations, and cognitive skills.

Wilbur described one play, in particular:

◄ Noteworthy for its simplicity, four girls use a curtain, two mats and two Easter baskets with plastic eggs to create their

top & bottom: Acrobatics in
the gym.

Voices of Children

story. It opens with two girls lying on the mats. They yawn, stretch out, close their eyes and pretend to go to sleep. From behind the curtain, out hop the other two acting as Easter bunnies with baskets; they place several eggs beside the sleeping girls and hop away. The children awake, surprised and delighted with their treasure. The girls fall asleep again and the bunnies return and add more eggs, then vanish behind the curtain. This takes place through three scenic variations.

In this seemingly simple, compressed form, the authors have expressed a story that captures the audience's interest by bringing them in on the gag of knowing what is causing the appearance of eggs, an event that is baffling to the characters who discover them. This is a sophisticated concept, an imaginative staging, a metaphor for life's mysteries.

Out of this open-space activity, in two years, they had developed a sense of form and an increased use of dramatic tension to sustain interest and that is the basis of any good drama or entertainment. ►

The children's spirits were always high around the shows and they often chose humorous topics. After announcing a fake weather report, the announcer might warn: "Stay indoors today, or high winds could blow you away," or "We are expecting heavy rains, so make sure you carry your umbrella." Allan played the role of a columnist modeled on the advice-dispensing Ann Landers. To the delight of his audience, he liked to stand on a table reading letters he made up with improvised remedies for the troubled. Harry and Alice performed sight gags, such as a customer getting angry at a waiter who poured coffee into a bottomless cup held over another cup.

Boys and girls worked together as performers and "stage hands." They prepared and moved sets, turned lights on and off, shone flashlights, rattled objects, and slammed doors to furnish sound effects. They created announcements and spread the word of the time and location a performance was to take place. Students and staff gathered to view the presentation and cheer for the performers.

Wilbur comments on the significance of dramatic play:

◄ The basic story themes are constant. Children transform themselves into a bad or a good parent, good or bad guys,

The Arts: A Child's First Language

winners and losers. The specifics shift with the times and culture. Prior to recent wars and ventures into space, the hero in children's stories was typically the cowboy. Then "Hi, ho, Silver!" was exchanged for "Blast off!" In past times, girls primarily played mothers, teachers, and nurses; now, doctors, astronauts, politicians.

Moving from spontaneous play to formal drama mirrors the historical birth of drama from ritual to staged presentation. There is a natural progression from the simplicity and diversity of dramatic play to the coherence and order of structured forms of drama as children learn about sequencing presentations, reading their scripts, and acting them out with grace and beauty before an audience. This evolving pattern can be observed with children everywhere. Dramatic play is not an escape, but a method of learning by doing. Our environment provided the opportunity for dramatic presentations on many levels. ►

Through language, music, and body movement, the performers communicated with each other and their audiences. In the process, they practiced and learned the skills required for self-discipline, organization, and critical appreciation. A significant part of their work was their recognition that what they did was important and that they could convey this for the enjoyment of their audience. In Kant's words, they had become "a community of appreciators."

During our four years at the school, the children continued to improvise spontaneous scenarios, as well as to work on their dramatic productions. The cooperative effort between students and teachers we had experienced with the creation of "Lost in Commercials" had become an integral part of our school's functioning.

The last play I remember was called "Wilbur Wilbur," a humorous interpretation of school life, with several skits. The children had become playwrights, actors, acrobats, dancers and singers, producers and critics. Their minds and imaginations had found words and expressions to create abstractions, stories, and songs told in their authentic voices and shared with like-minded spirits.

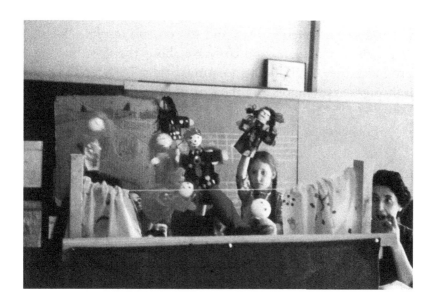

Puppet play.

The Arts: A Child's First Language

The Arts Form a Bridge

With their minds and bodies, the young artists invented shapes, colors, structures, songs, and dances, filling their school with the joy and energy of creation. They experienced the pleasure of creating and learning new things, and with their practice, discussions, and sharing ideas with peers and teachers improved their skills.

Working in the arts, the children learned to observe, to imagine and express their personal images, to hypothesize, to make judgments, and predict outcomes. Because they were invested and took pleasure in their activities, they learned to take risks by experimenting, to persevere and sustain their efforts, and to evaluate results. As children conceptualize, articulate, and converse about their art making and its products, they are building a natural bridge between their expression through art symbols and their developing language proficiency.

The Arts: A Child's First Language

Voices of Children

I love the moon

I love it so much

That I can kiss it

I love it more

And more

Everyday.

The Arts: A Child's First Language

[Children] learn when they are engaged in what they are learning and when the teacher is involved in it, too.
They learn about written language, mathematical relationships, and especially about the social and natural worlds.

– Virginia Casper and Rachel Theilheimer

Chapter 4

Reading, Writing and Mathematics

Living systems, from cells to societies, communicate through a variety of signals. Over millennia, humans developed a signal system of spoken and written words, along with the arts, to communicate information, thoughts, and emotions. Young children communicate through gestures, sounds, and the arts. By listening, observing, and imitating their parents' speech, and along with their guidance, children gradually learn to speak and structure a spoken and written language. By handling and sorting objects and creating patterns, children also become familiar with number concepts.

Language as Developing Thought

Lev Vygotsky has observed and written about the language development of children. He theorizes that children are born with the basic materials for intellectual development and that their abilities to pay attention, to experience sensation, to perceive and memorize, enable them to be actively involved in their own learning and discovery. Exercising these functions in a social context (with adults and peers) stimulates children to gain new understandings of their world and to develop their thought processes. The give and take of communicating with others provides the scaffolding for them to create a symbol system connecting words, objects, and ideas.

Wilbur wrote about how children begin to communicate and how this lays the foundation for the literacy skills they develop later:

◄ Beginning in the crib, young children experiment with sounds and words and invent a variety of monologues to accompany their play, sometimes using rhyming chants. The way children play and learn has a long history through time and cultures. Games, songs, stories and rhymes, such as Three Little Pigs, Eensie Weensie Spider, and Hickory Dickery Dock, are part of the tradition of poetic expression we use to reinforce language patterns and development. "Peek-a-boo, where's the baby? Oh, there you are!" brings giggles and pleasurable movement. It is the signing that precedes speech.

The spoken word, the written word, and human behavior depicted graphically are ordinarily presumed to have their locus within the territory of the "cognitive domain." Observation of the infant, however, suggests that communication with others is one mode of biologically rooted pleasure, a way children expand into the world. It starts with the infant's responding to the expressions and movements of those around her, at first spontaneously, then with increasing intent, pleasure, and maturity.

Stories move the play into another dimension: narrative. This is not dissimilar to the discoveries children make in their development in graphics—going from the abstraction of scribbles and shapes to representation, and from delineation to description. ►

When children learn to speak, they continue their monologues. By joining thoughts to words, they interpret the world and their activities to themselves. Vygotsky has termed this talking out loud to oneself "inner speech" and describes how children create dialogues with imaginary characters and develop narratives for planning and solving problems. By around age seven children generally speak fluently, develop conversational skills, and tell stories about their lives and interests. Inner speech disappears as they become able to think silently to themselves.

As children play with words and hear and tell stories, they both create and derive meaning. From early on, children grasp that stories they hear or see in books are symbolic, metaphoric expressions. Without articulating these ideas, they know they can imagine and invent their own metaphors and symbols, such as stories and artworks. They can begin to grasp that letters and numbers are parts of a symbol system that stands for sounds, words, and quantities.

Literacy

In our world of the last few hundred years, literacy has largely replaced the oral traditions people used in the past to communicate and transmit knowledge and culture. With the advent of the printing press and the requirement for literacy in all aspects of life, masses of people obtained access to print materials.

To read and write, children must be able to decipher the symbol systems undergirding literacy and correlate the abstract visual symbols of the alphabet and the words they spell with spoken language. In turn, they have to read these constructs and derive meaning from them.

In math, they must correlate a physical quantity with a numeric symbol, as well as the word that is equivalent to that symbol, e.g., the numeral 9 stands for a quantity, and the word "nine" does as well. They have to know how to manipulate the relationships between numbers, as in addition and the other numerical operations. When children have learned to speak, they are ready to master the skills required for language and mathematical literacy.

Philosophy of Language:
Teaching and Learning

From the time that literacy became important for functioning in society, thinkers and educators have grappled with pedagogies for teaching reading and writing, as well as math, and schools have adopted a variety of methods.

Lev Vygotsky (1978) wrote about requirements for learning.

"When it comes to language learning, the authenticity of the environment and the affinity between the participants are essential elements to make the learner feel part of this environment. Those elements are rarely predominant in conventional classrooms."

Wilbur's thoughts follow here:

◄ The sticky wicket of this is not only that of teaching basic skills, but doing this within a context, an environment that

Reading, Writing and Mathematics

promotes not only the desire in all children to have mastery, but in such ways that associations of satisfaction, yes, even delight, are established in the process. Reading and writing not as a chore, but as a vast storehouse of present and future pleasure. ➤

Creating a Language Learning Program

To support the children's acquisition of literacy, we decided to use an eclectic approach. We used *The Language Arts Program*, first developed in the early progressive schools, and based on the concept that reading and writing are meaningful experiences for children.

We combined this program with phonics instruction, which involves decoding a word by its sounds. With the children's own language as a base, we set out to construct a program from which they could expand their learning. To implement this, we combined teacher-directed activities with open-ended methodologies:

We organized study groups to assist with reading and writing skills. In these we used instructional methods, such as the Look/Say or Sight Words method for recognizing/memorizing words by sight, and phonics. When needed, we used phonics recordings, cards, and charts. We created worksheets with exercises geared to the children's level. Together we made dictionaries and pictionaries to define and illustrate words of interest from books or the children's own stories. From these words, new sentences and stories grew. When guinea pigs were born or we visited the Statue of Liberty, we solicited and wrote the children's observations on a large sheet of paper. We displayed these experience charts where the children could see and read them.

To help the children create their own materials, we used a mimeograph machine (copier of the time) to print stories, which became reading matter for the group. The symbols created by individuals became part of their social experience. We tape-recorded music and discussions. The teachers and children frequently communicated with each other, and the children had opportunities to read and write about a variety of topics. When the children developed their spontaneous dramatic and puppet plays into presentations for an audience, we helped them to write scripts that could be used for new productions. They made pictures and signs for their various projects, decorated letters of the alphabet, and printed with a rubber alphabet and carved erasers. Language activities played an ongoing role in the children's lives at school, in an environment where reading, writing, speaking, listening, and viewing were integral to daily life.

Wilbur wrote about learning:

◄ The question is how to teach the skills in a way that infuses the learning process with the child's inherent use and love of language and story.

At the center of our program are the stories and accounts the children tell and write, cartoons in which they combine graphics and words, reports for the class newspaper, *The Squeaker Times*, whose content is chosen and written or dictated by the children. They learn to read not only their own written word, but also that of peers and other literature. They can find books on a broad range of subjects in the class library and create their own books. They can browse, read and listen to stories, engage in free dramatic play, and improvise songs and skits.

When children feel ownership in the process of learning, their writing will reflect the depiction of *their* here and now, of external/internal experience. They will perceive reading and writing as a pleasure, rather than a dull task. ►

Telling and Sharing Stories

From their early years, children narrate imaginative stories to themselves as well as to their pets and toys. They instruct dolls and cats, direct toy trucks and planes, and talk to others about events in their lives. In school, the children talked freely about their interests, their families, their pets, and world events. By listening and responding, we encouraged them to expand their natural storytelling abilities and attempts at writing.

Reading, Writing and Mathematics

We might have said, "That's an interesting story, maybe we can all hear it, let's write it down." A child could write independently, or a teacher might help with spelling or the child's dictated story. What is told can be written. When children tell, write, and discuss their stories, they can inspire their classmates to find their own ideas they wish to express. Thus, stories become seeds for the imagination.

Topics and Content of Children's Writing

Wilbur wrote about children's writing:
➤ The stories the children told, and their creations through dramatic play, cartoons, and skits, were mostly about understanding of relationships. They dealt with being "bossed" and punishment and with emotions such as distrust, dominance, anxiety, fear, anger, and sadness, as well as longing, love and joy, and the peaceful kindness and genuine charm of amicable families where children are accepted.

The children also wrote about factual experiences, describing basic life functions, such as eating and bodily processes. The passage of day and night, dreams, and the indefatigable unconscious and subconscious, affect their stories. Welling up from the depths, the children's emotions spilled out in the metaphoric forms of their stories. They told them again and again, seeking clarification, affirmation, and input from the audience. Repetition of a deeply felt experience proves to have healing power. In stories, the children could find creative ways of overcoming frightful situations and felt safe knowing that, in their tales, these feelings exist only in their fantasies.

In his book *Fantasy and Distancing*, Arthur N. Applebee (1978) writes about how separating the story, both in place and time, from the children's actual reality, makes it possible for them to explore the aesthetic experience, knowing that there will be no consequences in their real world.

Teachers can suggest specific topics such as "the scariest day of my life" for wonderful and important stories, or we can elicit ideas by reading stories depicting genuine strong feelings, both positive and negative.

By discussing experiences of fear in *Charlotte's Web*, Toad's braggadocio in *Wind in the Willows*, and Max's relief at being back home in *Where the Wild Thing Are*, we can evoke themes for stories that relate to the children's own lives. They also read and wrote imaginary stories with symbolic fictional characters in the form of animals and monsters, as in The Paint Blob and Frankastorus and Dr. Broncato (below).

Storytelling, similar to other aspects of the child's life in the creative endeavors of the arts, is charged with multiple sources that feed the sense of well-being. It is much more than mastery of symbols and words. It is an individual's creative expression moving outward to establish community, communication, and mastery of the culture's expressive forms. Children construct their stories with candor, receptivity, and daring assertions of "the way it is." ►

Story content ranged far and wide and, in keeping with our goal of fostering children's' interests, we did not exclude topics, such as space exploration and dinosaurs or comic books the children brought. At that time, these were banned from most schools as teachers saw their powerful pull on children's imaginations as competitors with studies of the here and now or more recent past. Today, Ray Bradbury and other writers have made science fiction acceptable as a literary genre. Comics are not always frowned upon, and at Columbia University, Michael Bitz has developed The Comic Book Project to reinforce literacy skills.

The children drew illustrations for their stories, and those not yet able to write, dictated them to their teachers.

Wilbur wrote about introducing children to writing:

◄ As children learn to write in the first years of school, there is usually a gap between their verbal skills and their abilities to write and record their thoughts. In the early years, the adult can write out the children's spoken stories and avoid their being frustrated in trying to put thoughts on paper

Reading, Writing and Mathematics

```
Once upon a time there was a monster. His
name was Frankastorus. And there was a
professor. And his name was Dr. Boncato.
BBB Dr. Boncato made a formula to kill
the monster. He put in acide in his squir
ting bottle And he put it in his formula
bottle.  Then he took his formula bottle
to put it in his special heater . He turned
on the heater to grind the formula he put
in the funnel. Then he took the funnel
and poured a drop into the pot and it
smaoked up.  Then he poured it into his
special acid bottle. Then he put it in
his special water pistol gun ( It shoots
all kind of formulas )/.
        Then he went ou+side and he saw the
monster with five pointed teeth and he had
six claws three on each hand. And then Dr.
Boncato took his gun and fired at the monst
er.  And the monster died and everybody
lived happily ever after.
```

Frankastorous and Dr. Boncatos
A story about conquering a monster through ingenuity.
The eternal battle of good and evil.

with limited writing skills. By recording the children's dictated stories, we reinforce the connection between speech and writing. Children are aware that we are there to facilitate their learning via the extensions of symbolizations in drawing, painting, dramatics, and language expressions.

Through reading and writing their own and other's stories, children learn the skills of decoding, grammar, punctuation, and syntax needed for literacy. Frequent verbal exchanges and use of print materials provided opportunities for the children to connect letters and words to the meanings they conveyed. Hearing coherent spoken narratives and being read to set the base for the child's love of the word and literature. ➤

Storytelling

Wilbur was a consummate storyteller, and the children loved listening to him. He made up his own stories and led the children into contributing to his tales as he told them. He attributed his interest to his Southern heritage with its tradition of personal story telling:

Wilbur described this process:

◄ How did I become a storyteller to children, not just of stories I had heard, but of my own fabrication? By the most subtle, gratifying way of learning. I learned by absorbing ideas from my mentors, such as the caring middle school English teacher Miss Raglan, and hearing the renowned storyteller, Dean William Faulkner, recounting folk stories from his book, *The Days When Animals Talked*. I learned from family friends and my father, who told his Pa tales of growing up on a Texas cattle ranch. My Uncle James told about his Civil War experiences and my Grandma Rogers of her life in the West with the railroad builders of the mid 1800's.

Reading tales, short stories, novels, biographies, and autobiographies in youth and adulthood was a central pleasure and occupation of my leisure hours. I was engaged in the

Reading, Writing and Mathematics

compelling world revealed in literature, a world whose insights are rarely shown in the context of life.

These experiences made me curious about how people used words, how they conversed, how they expressed themselves. When I began teaching, this heritage contributed to my appreciation of children's verbal and graphic expressions and their dramatic play. Their inventiveness and use of fantasy inspired me to develop my own imagination and story-telling skills. ►

Wilbur's experience in the environment of free-flowing language exchanges is another example of how learning takes place in social settings where people share knowledge and interests without preset goals. Everyone cooperates, and everyone benefits. At Bank Street, Wilbur was influenced by his teacher, Claudia Lewis, who pioneered the recognition of the originality and literary value of children's expressions. He thought about the meaning of what children were saying and analyzed the themes in their stories for his Master's thesis.

Most afternoons at our school, Wilbur told an improvised tale he called, "The Baby Story," and the kids would go around the building announcing, "Hurry up, Wilbur's going to tell 'The Baby Story!' Most would eagerly come to listen. As the story unfolded, Wilbur created drawings and cartoons with dialogue to illustrate it and enrolled the kids to contribute their own interpretations. Throughout each day, children read, listened to, told, and wrote stories. Stories were everywhere.

Wilbur wrote:

◄ In this early stage of schooling, children are filled with delight, laughter, and admiration for the creativity of peers. They regard learning to read as one of the things kids do, like drawing and painting pictures, cuddling the guinea pig, frolicking with playmates, playing "Space" in the gym, drawing houses and faces on the sidewalk, playing hide-and-go-seek, and building castles in the sand. We often hear, "I like to do it" or "It's fun," which is to say that children experience pleasurable emotion in the process of doing and learning. ►

top & bottom: Wilbur tells and illustrates
"The Baby Story."

Reading, Writing and Mathematics

Cartoons as Reading Material

Wilbur wrote about the content and stages of cartoons and stories:

◄ Children frequently drew cartoons on their own and enjoyed the ones I improvised with them for my "Baby Story." With their predominant pictorial content and simple caption structure of balloons, containing as little as one word, the cartoons constitute a bridge between a drawing and a story with discernable narrative. By joining simple words and graphics, beginning readers easily created cartoons. As in their stories, the children dealt with the subjects of wars, monsters, space, current events and family life and their power relationships. They depicted joy, sadness, conflicts, and fears, relying frequently on humor to anesthetize the sting of painful experience.

We realized that, with their language content, the cartoons could serve as a reading material, and we encouraged the children to make copies for the class. Over time we observed stages in the development of cartoon structures.

It starts with the simple frame that is concurrent with the story, presenting a basic situation and comments. The child draws a picture and writes the legend, or asks the adult for assistance. It is usually a descriptive sentence that in words repeats the action or image above, but does not develop it in any way. Its most obvious features are simplicity and immediacy.

When Eric read about the Revolutionary War, he created a cartoon summing up his feelings about it. Though his title "A Cartoon All about the Revolutionary War" is a bit of a hyperbole, he understands that two military forces are locked in a struggle against each other. In the face-off between the American and British ships of war, as signified by their flags and legends, Eric expresses his sympathies for the Americans by having the British cannonball miss its mark and fall harmlessly into the water.

The American taunts from his still-solid deck, "Nie Nie," and Eric celebrates the victory of the underdog, perhaps projecting his own response to conflicts. He understands the rid-

Eric's cartoon all about the Revolutionary War.

Reading, Writing and Mathematics

Earl the Octopus.

icule incurred when a powerful enemy misses an easy mark, and the emotions of derision and anger in the two captains confronting each other.

Note the exclamation points on the British side: Eric wants us to know that he is no mere six-year-old child and places the numerals 6¾ after his name. Eric was able to express complex ideas in the simple construct of the one-frame cartoon.

Many children drew one-frame cartoons and expanded their expressions to cartoons with additional frames with story lines. The cartoons are not illustrations for stories but constitute the story itself.

In Earl Octopus, Anthony depicts a complex story in a multi-frame cartoon. He shows a sophisticated sense of the world and its machinations. Earl Octopus, pictured as a shady cigar-smoking character with a smug expression, counts his ill-gotten money and is devastated when most of it is removed by a bulldozer fish sent by the Tax Department.

Laura's multi-frame vignette is not intended to be humorous; rather, she tells a story of daily life and friendship. In this form of cartooning, there is no dialogue, only captions describing the actions in the illustrations. The words and images convey the warmth the friends feel for each other, and the language is poetic: "She wakes up so quick, like thunder." A teacher typed her dictated text.

An unknown author depicts the history of music in a sophisticated four-frame cartoon. Note the band is named The Cavemen. In each frame a couple is dancing: In Caveman, the couple, oddly, is dressed in ordinary modern clothes. In Old Man—meaning pre-historic—a woman dances with what seems to be a horse. Both have happy expressions, perhaps signaling a close human/animal connection. In both, the couples are holding hands.

In NOW MAN and NEW MAN, the couple's clothes are elaborated and each partner dances in his/her own space without an orchestra. The lines drawn around them indicate speeded-up rhythms. The figures in NOW MAN anticipate the abbreviated fashions of our day. The cartoon expresses

Laura's cartoon.

History of Music.

Reading, Writing and Mathematics

The Paint Monster

This is a picture of the paint monster and
the man

BrCeLIA

A man was in a paint factory. He was making
paint and he spilled a little turpentine into a bucket
of red paint. Then he spilled some blue paint, green
and white paint into the bucket. He thought this was
pretty, so he started to stir the paint up and suddenly
his dog ran into the room and knocked the bucket
of paint over. The man was very mad at
the dog so he locked the dog up in the other
room. Oh well! said the man I will make some
more. But suddenly he looked down at the floor
and saw that the big blob of paint was moving
The man was not scared, he wondered and wondered
what could have happened.

left & right: Celia's Paint Monster.

The Paint Monster (continued)

Then the man remembered he had spilled a little turpentine into the bucket, but he said, "What can a little turpentine do?" Then he noticed that the blob of paint was right behind him. But he was still not scared. So he started to think and think what could have made the paint blob come to life. But anyhow he was now scared, so he ran as fast as he could go. The paint blob showered thousands of little crops of paint all over his factory. But then the man looked at the wall and he noticed it was very beautiful and he wondered what was doing it. Then he remembered about the blob. He stopped running and said to the blob "I want to be your friend." But the blob didn't know what the man was thinking, that he could make hundreds of dollars by painting people's walls with the blob.

And they lived happily ever after in a paint factory.

Celia

the author's perception of the passage of time, the changes that have taken place in relationships, and the tempo of different periods.

We observe that around the ages of eight or nine, as, with time and practice, children's abilities mature, they expand their narratives to elaborate on the predominant point. The child now conceives of the written word as representing independent thoughts: the content and the language of the story no longer accompany the visual image; they are central. The visual image illustrates not the total story, but one aspect, until the word story finally emerges on its own without any illustration.

There are several exceptions; some children, for whatever reasons, prefer depicting events visually, through illustration and cartoons, to writing the story, and will continue in this way for some time. Others will sometimes use cartoons—usually for humorous content—for one occasion and stories for another. There is not always a straight line from stage to stage, and some will use overlapping styles. Some, in the latter years of the primary grades, with their own increasing competency in the skill of writing, will go primarily to the written stories.

The cartoons the children produced possessed clarity, complexity, and insightfulness, while remaining childlike in the best sense of the word. Through their images and dialogues, the cartoonists expressed a range of emotions and sophisticated perceptions about their world. While engaged in creating cartoons, stories, and reports, the children were not aware that they were improving their reading and writing skills. ►

Making and Using
Signs, Labels and Posters

Making signs was another purposeful literacy activity the children enjoyed. They made signs and labels, such as THE MUSEUM OF BABY DINOSAURS, or DANGER ZONE, with information about their block buildings and wood and collage constructions. They needed posters for school events and staged plays, elections, and radio and TV shows. We helped by sounding out the letters so the kids could write on their own or made copies from notes they had dictated to us. Because these signs were integral to the children's activities, and their messages communicated relevant information, children were strongly motivated to read and understand them.

Conversations

Wilbur wrote:

◄ Most important, we recognized, was the spoken word, free and fluent. As children and teachers engaged in open-ended discussions and dialogues, they communicated personal and meaningful content. The children could express and create their own language experiences.

Following is an example of a candid discussion in which the kids raised questions about adult behavior.

The children and I are dismantling the defunct typewriter donated by a parent. Sasha studies me for a moment before deciding to broach the subject.

"Wilbur, could I ask you something? Why are you so nervous?"

Sasha's question catches me off guard. Liz comes to my aid.

"It's because he smokes. Smoking makes grown-ups that way."

Darby, the skeptic, objects. "My uncle jumps like anything. And he doesn't smoke."

Reading, Writing and Mathematics

Mimeograph print.

Margaret removes a spring from the typewriter with a pair of pliers. "My Dad smokes cigars! Yucky! The smell gets all over the place."

"Grown-ups," philosopher Danny explains, "can't help it. They gotta have their little *whatchamacallits*, their little nibbling things."

"Pacifiers," says Sasha. "They're called 'pacifiers.'"

"Yeah, they're called pacifiers."

"Looka quick!" Danny exclaims. "I printed my name!" He points to the impression of type keys on his arm.

"When I grow up, I'm going to get a tattoo. For my birthday." ►

The children felt safe in probing the behavior of their teacher, from which they drew inferences as to its causes and attempted to reach conclusions about the behavior of adults in general.

"They gotta have their little *whatchamacallits*, their little nibbling things."

In their own words, the children philosophized about the nature of addiction, and we returned to the theme at other times. In this open forum, the children and teachers exchanged meaningful thoughts and ideas about their lives and the world.

The Mimeograph Machine and the Tape Recorder

Teachers and children used the media of the day to record and share experiences and events. While the children could easily access ready-made materials, like commercial books and magazines, the mimeograph machine made it possible to produce their own literary creations, duplicate, and disseminate them.

Wilbur described the experience:

◄ The setting contains a classroom library with attractive, easy readers and an array of picture and storybooks. In one corner of the room, the mimeograph machine, aka the Spirit Duplicator, awaits the children. With this copying machine

Reading, Writing and Mathematics

of the time, they can create multiple copies from a stencil. In baskets we have placed nearby, they can find the paper, stencils, pens and pencils they need to prepare their materials for printing.

When Lynn wanted to make her own poster for electing a Troll City mayor, she chose a stencil from the box with red, green, blue, and purple blanks. Pressing down with a ballpoint pen, she drew a picture of the candidate.

"Wilbur, how do you spell promise?"

I helped her by sounding out the word and except for the silent e she was able to form it on her own. For beginning writers, I would usually write their dictated text in print letters on the stencil, so it could be easily read. After Lynn placed the stencil on the machine, I stood by as she cranked the handle to make prints. Some children did eventually learn to do the process on their own, though the inks running and drying were always a problem. Through the day, we produced a variety of prints, and children printed the desired number, enough to take a few home and some for each child and teacher in the group. They distributed the documents, and children responded according to the mood of the day, the intensity of their play at the moment, and their genuine appreciation. We saved some prints for books we made with the children for the class library. The teachers responded by describing a particular feature or aspect of their work:

"Um, look at the careful way you drew the frog."

"I know what you mean."

"Now, where in the world do you get such weird ideas?" said in an approving manner (Wilbur's humor).

The work is accepted for what it is, no matter how seemingly simple, odd, banal, or sophisticated—a genuine, unique, graphic expression of the child. The teachers made no comparisons between the children's work. From each according to his ability, to each according to his need. Hmmm… sounds familiar? ▶

By producing and publishing their own print materials, the young authors participated in creating our culture's most valued vehicles for disseminating information and ideas.

On a bulky reel-to-reel tape recorder we recorded stories, songs. and discussions such as the one on addiction previously noted. We equipped it with tapes, and many kids learned to work it on their own. Sometimes they moved it near their block buildings to narrate events such as preparing for an imaginary space liftoff or the birth of guinea pigs.

Wilbur wrote about the recordings:

◄ Alison, Sara, and Kathy asked to have their improvised song taped. It is a parody of an exercise in their reader, and they call it the Reader Song. They delivered the song in a tone of glee, aware of the humor in their reinterpreting the repetitive text of the exercise. For several rounds they improvise variations, and I am drawn into their mood. Each time they sang, we engaged in a humorous repartee about their composing the song in secret. While listening to the children's tapes, I found one on which three boys engaged in a repartee of scatological words and phrases. They had moved the tape recorder to a small room away from everyone. ►

Interestingly, the boys had the social awareness to realize that their expressions were not acceptable in a public forum. By isolating themselves with the tape recorder, they found a safe outlet for their "forbidden" thoughts. We do not know whether they meant to erase the tape or replay it to themselves and/or a selected audience.

Wilbur wrote in his article "Experience and Creative Language" (1975) that "Vulgarity and coarseness are a part of the language of childhood. Adults should know enough about this not to interfere too much with it, while encouraging other forms of expression."

The tape recorder and spirit duplicator provided structures for sharing and preserving many of the children's verbal expressions and, in Wilbur's words, "pluck language from its evaporation upon pronouncement and give it a presence beyond the moment."

Using the reel-to-reel tape recorder, Louis recorded information about the space station he made from blocks. To represent the station's machinery, he used cassettes and electric circuitry plates we

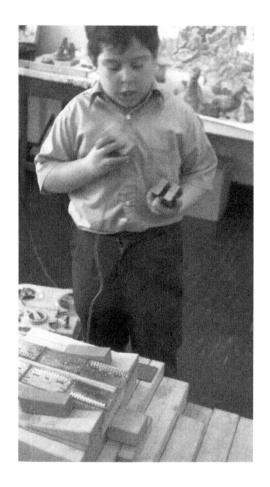

Recording a story about the
space station.

Voices of Children

purchased from industrial surplus stores on Canal Street in lower Manhattan. Louis looked to be deeply involved in explaining his imaginative construct and exemplified Wilbur's thoughts about self-directed learning: "Working, creating are keystones for rational behavior, and in the sense of being self-chosen, self-directed, self-regulatory, the child can take pleasure in the accomplishment."

These next few sections describe how the children cooperated during sustained group efforts to create structures for communicating with their classmates, the school, and beyond. The results reflected their interest and enthusiasm and were appreciated by their audience.

Children Create Their Library

Sometime during our first year, our group visited a library, where we learned to use the filing system. Soon after, Alison, Liz, and Laura hatched the idea of creating their own library in the Art Room. In a corner of the room, they stocked an old shelf we found with their school-made books, commercial publications, and magazines. A small wood table became their reference desk, and various "librarians" took turns cataloguing the inventory. They made file cards, and we found rubber stamps they used for loans and returns. It was like a neighborhood library where people browse, borrow, and return books and consult the librarians for selections. Most everyone took part in using and working in the library during its hours of operation, posted on a sign. As authors, and now, librarians, the children were connected to books in a direct, personal way.

The library was one of the children's dramatic scenarios, enacted over time, and they were responsible for the initiative, logistics, and sustained organization and development of the enterprise. Everyone was interested and had fun creating and using the library. We, the teachers, were on call to assist with materials and support. It was an example of authentic child expression, of children's powers to imagine and cooperate in complex experiences.

Reading, Writing and Mathematics

I do not recall the titles of books made by the students or myself, but some of the titles of Wilbur's homemade books included the following:

The Baby Story: Wilbur's ongoing tale of the adventures of a magical baby, told with the children.

One Day in the Life of Wrigley's Chewing Gum and Daring Detective Bubble Yum: Two books Wilbur developed using collage and drawing centered on chewing gum.

Signs We See: Collage and writing about signs in our environment.

My Story: Wilbur's autobiography through photos and narrative.

The School Newspaper

During our second year, the popular school newspaper, *The Squeaker Times*, emerged. It became a vehicle through which the children communicated about life in and out of school.

Wilbur wrote about its inception:

◄ One day, while we were using the mimeograph machine, Louis (six years old) said, "This can make lots of copies, maybe we could make a newspaper."

"That's a good idea, Louis, let's work on it."

Louis told several of his friends and they and Rachel set about creating the paper.

I shall never forget the bemused faces of David and Chris who, when the paper was launched, immediately rushed to obtain pencil and pad as befitted reporters, and then left the room in a rush lest they miss some hot "scoop" taking place in the school. They returned a few minutes later with the announcement that they didn't know how to write. Indeed, they could not, and I doubt very much if until that moment the advantages of print had seriously concerned them. In time, of course, they did learn to read and write.

For the moment, Rachel worked out a system of reporting giving them full status as reporters. They made simple drawings, or lined notations to record their story, and Rachel

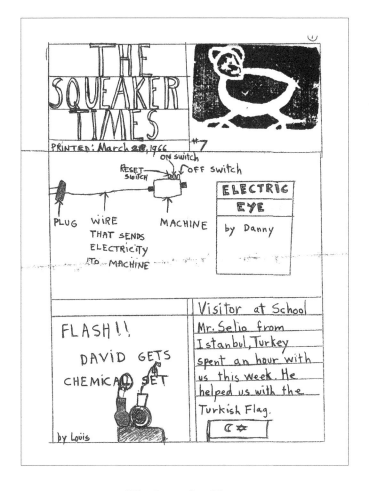

The Squeaker Times.

Reading, Writing and Mathematics

left + right: Invented symbols.
Triangles are barrels and the round shapes on top are peas.
Stick figures are kids.

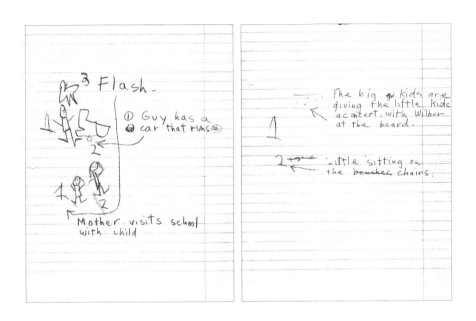

³ Flash.

① Guy has a
② car that runs ③

Mother visits school
with child

The big kids are
giving the little kids
a concert, with Wilbur
at the board.

2 Little sitting on
the ~~benches~~ chairs.

translated these into appropriate words. Anyone in the group might become a reporter by declaring her/himself to be one. They felt confident to play their roles and learned the required tasks on the job. Sometimes they took a name to fit the role; Bob, Joe, Jane and Tobor were some.

Thus, if the "drawing record" (previous page) is unclear to the viewer in and of itself, it becomes immediately clear when we read Rachel's notation: "The little kids are picking peas out of one barrel and putting them into another barrel." Tobor, our reporter in this case, has reported a "happening" that apparently constitutes a news event. "Little kids," by the way, are children younger than oneself, in this case the four- and five-year-olds. ►

The reporters frequently used this symbol system, in which they combined stick figures and shapes with letters and numbers. They grasped the concept that their pictographs were abstract symbols, but they did not develop a unified system. Each created individual images to represent his experiences. The invented writing served to communicate while the children worked on mastering the recognized symbol system. Some dictated news items to the teacher, and as time went on, they contributed pieces that they wrote independently.

After much thought and deliberation, the kids named the paper *The Squeaker Times*, inspired by the squeaking communications of the beloved family of guinea pigs that lived with us. Someone made a carving of a guinea pig on a large, rubber eraser, which we printed on the masthead of each issue.

Wilbur described how the paper functioned:

◄ *The Squeaker Times* was a joint labor of love of Rachel and the children. Rachel was the "chief" as Louis put it, operating as copy person, editor, and guide. Early in the paper's advent, Rachel and the kids decided on two basic rules: the first was that since the paper was to be distributed to any adult or child in or out of school who requested a copy, no news would be printed that hurt a person's feelings; the other, that anyone mentioned in the paper would be asked for permission to use his/her name. The paper was published whenever enough "news" accumulated or when special events took place. ►

The newspaper differed from the books we made by collating individual stories; it was a sustained group effort through which we welded a variety of items into a cohesive whole.

Wilbur wrote about the paper's special qualities:

◄ Much of the conversation of children is in the form and content of news and commentaries on recent events in their lives. What would we expect primary school children to report, assuming the news was to be placed in a class newspaper? If the paper had merit, it would give us a sense of life in a particular classroom or school. If the class were lively, the paper could be spirited and humorous and bristle with the events taking place. It would have some of the graphic pull of a comic book, not in its subject matter, but in the way in which the visual conglomerate would attract the eye. It would be an open, rather than closed, expression and would reflect the children's spontaneous use of language.

The quality of the material would vary a great deal since we know that even a group of children of the same chronological age has a developmental range difference of several years. For children of this age (6-7), news statements would generally be brief. Graphics such as drawings, illustrations, and cartoons would figure predominantly, as the skills in these areas are generally more developed for six- or seven-year-old children, than are their abilities in writing. Children of this age play graphically with words and create designs with letters and the space around them. These would add some pleasant touches to enhance the paper's visual appeal.

Reporting a story can help children to develop their critical function of thought. They can find and create the appropriate metaphors for actual events—the war in Vietnam, or weather disasters, such as hurricanes. They will be able to imagine the actual event and to reduce it to the comprehensible, sometimes by the devices of humor, and diminish its overwhelming consequences—in short, to recreate an actual experience through images that they can grasp and incorporate.

Reading, Writing and Mathematics

Humor serves important functions and often, in *The Squeaker Times*, visual and verbal jokes are used in a spirit of fun and exuberance. In fact, there were once three dogs in the school office, by invitation. But none of them, as far as we know, were debauched on booze and cigars as depicted in Alan's cartoon "Rent" (opposite page). The actual can be dallied with, and playfulness can beget creativity.

What stands out in all this is the texture of life in school. It is evident from the data supplied within *The Squeaker Times*, from the reporting of the many activities taking place, that an approximation, at least, of life outside the school and life inside the school has taken place.

Caring does indeed follow upon loving, and the warmth that is expressed in *The Squeaker Times* suggests that mutuality. ►

The Squeaker Times was a vivid example of the relevance of the written language through which the children transmitted information and ideas. It was a creative, cooperative endeavor, in which children found expression for the factual and imaginary stories they wanted to share, and both reflected and influenced communication within the school.

Headlines from *The Squeaker Times* included: MORE GUINEA PIGS, DINOSAUR PAGE, LITTLE KID ACTIVITIES, MAGNIFIED NEWS, PLANT NEWS: HOW TO GROW AN AVOCADO, SPORTS NEWS, DANCE SHOW IN THE GYM, and REPORT FROM THE SCIENCE CLUB.

Horrorscope

One day, Danny reported that some older boys had chased him in a subway station. Fortunately, he escaped unharmed, but he was very frightened. When he recounted the story in school, other children talked about frightening events and dreams they had experienced. "Danny, how about writing this down?" I suggested.

top & bottom: Three dogs in the office.

Reading, Writing and Mathematics

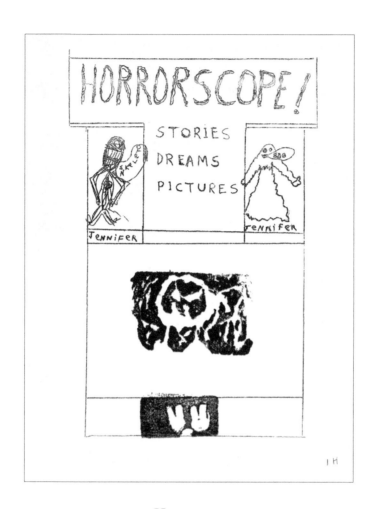

Horrorscope.

Voices of Children

"A Fright That Never Came Back."

The idea spread; other children wrote or dictated their fearsome tales, and some drew illustrations. Following our pattern of tell-write-print-read, we printed the stories on the mimeograph machine and assembled them into a booklet.

"These all sound like horror stories." someone called out.

"Let's call this the *Horrorscope*."

More children wanted to tell stories, and the *Horrorscope* group (open to anyone) met several times. They wrote and read their stories about scary happenings; some were true, and others involved fictional characters and events. We discussed the stories and the children's thoughts about them, and the *Horrorscope* became a forum and outlet where the children could express their fears and apprehensions. Eventually, they lost interest in the *Horrorscope*, and *The Squeaker Times* remained the school's main vehicle of communication.

Fostering an Ethos of Literacy

By creating *The Squeaker Times* and *Horrorscope*, the children practiced their skills in writing, reading, drawing, and observing. In these enterprises, they worked cooperatively and independently as engaged reporters, interviewers, writers, artists, editors, printers, distributors, and decision makers. They followed the inherent discipline required to produce these publications, and their pages made manifest the children's labor, skills, and high spirits. In addition to practicing their skills, the children gained understanding of the relation between reading/writing and the creation of meaningful content.

Though not everyone told stories or drew cartoons or painted, it is certain that everyone participated in some form of creative activity that had a language component. Dialoguing, reading, and writing were ongoing throughout the day and throughout the building, as well as during the more concentrated instructional periods.

By constant practice of all these activities, teachers and children together created a rich surround of verbal and print material. The children developed a familiarity with letters, their uses, shapes, and sounds. Eventually, they formed words and sentences reflecting their

Celia (right) and friends, in
dress up clothes.

Reading, Writing and Mathematics

thoughts and experiences and created structures for communicating these to others.

Graduate Celia Converse remembers the school's language arts activities:

"I credit it for teaching me to love books; it definitely did that. And teaching you to use your imagination. I remember we had our own little books that we put together. I remember writing poems and thinking that was great. This is how we learned English."

Mathematics

Some have called mathematics a universal language, as well as the language of science, and some have spoken of mathematics as art and poetry. It is a symbol system, which children need to learn in order to function in the world. In their everyday activities, children absorb basic math concepts the same way they learn to speak without formal instruction.

Lev Vygotsky (1978) in *Mind and Society* said that "Long before the time of first attending school, children have had some experience with quantity—they have had to deal with operations of division, addition, subtraction, and determination of size. Consequently, children have their preschool arithmetic, which only myopic psychologists ignore."

Wilbur concurred:

◄ Children learn starting with early games involving counting fingers and toes, such as This Little Piggy, stories like The Three Little Pigs and songs like London Bridge (subtraction) and daily events like setting plates on a table to match the number of people using them. Experiences like these help children absorb basic ideas, which form a familiar ground in which more formal concepts can develop. ►

To help the children with their math explorations, we created an environment with a range of activities that embodied math concepts embedded in daily life. We also offered a structured learning program.

The children liked to "guesstimate" weights and sizes and check them out by weighing and measuring themselves, as well as guinea pigs, objects, and plants. We noted and kept records of these and created graphs to compare and review changes as the plants, animals, and children grew. The children also weighed ingredients for cooking, measured wood for woodworking, and cloth and yarn for sewing and weaving. They made maps and charts to re-create trips in the neighborhood. The children enjoyed spending their allowances buying snacks at Hi and Mel's corner luncheonette, and handling money provided reinforcement of number concepts. In these operations, they were gaining skills in estimating, hypothesizing, calculating, and making judgments.

Wilbur expressed his thoughts on teaching and learning math concepts:

◄ Mathematical concepts exist in all facets of life, and experience with them forms an underlying construct that, unconsciously, helps in developing abstraction and generalization. Although when in school I took particular pride in being obtuse in arithmetic, I was okay to match pennies with the neighborhood kids, score the runs and innings of our baseball games, shoot dice, play Monopoly, and count the profits made from selling lukewarm soda pop from shacks constructed along main thoroughfares. We didn't know the word "circumference" in the first grade, but without it, we drew circles in the dirt with string and sticks tied to both ends.

The teacher's warning that failure to study brought inevitable retribution in the form of inability to earn one's living had little effect on the small neighborhood business that I had established. I took care of and fed hens that gratefully laid eggs I sold to neighbors.

School-taught measurements would never have been so tedious if teachers had remembered how, in their own childhoods, they'd marked off baseball fields in vacant lots by "giant steps" and built skate scooters and tree houses with all steps and planks sawed to the proper length. ►

Reading, Writing and Mathematics

Wilbur's childhood math experiences in Nashville, Tennessee, in the nineteen twenties and thirties, exist everywhere in different forms.

How We Used Math Materials

We used Cuisenaire Rods, a structural material, to help the children grasp mathematical relationships. The rods consist of wooden cubes ½-inch square and multiples thereof. Each rod's color and size correspond to a number. The children used these appealing colorful shapes to make buildings and abstract forms as well as to learn mathematical operations.

Wilbur described how we used Cuisenaire Rods:

◄ The children affectionately called the rods: ones-ees, twos-ees, threes-ees, etc., and, on their own, discovered that they have numerical relationships. I might propose: "Look, ten ones-ees make up a tens-ee, two fives-ees make up a tens-ee. Let's see how many other ways we can make ten." They realize that combining the one-unit block and the nine-unit block equals the ten-unit block. The same with the two-unit block and the eight-unit block, and on up. As the children continue to explore, they delight in their discoveries. They appreciate not only the mathematical connections but also, the array, the stately procession of the rods' seemingly inexhaustible permutations.

"Look, subtract one white from the four and one-fourth is missing, three-fourths remain."

We wrote out our findings in numerical symbols. The children grasped the connection between the concrete rods and abstract numbers as well as how to conduct operations with them. ►

Cuisenaire Rods

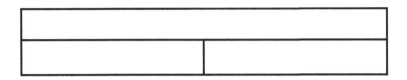

The ten-rod on top and two fives beneath is a graphic representation of the concepts of addition: 5 + 5 = 10, multiplication: 5 × 2 = 10 and division: 10 ÷ 5 = 2.

A Fifteenth Street School graduate once said, "I remember building stuff with them, learning with them, loving the colors and the logic to the system, and I remember the colors and corresponding number values of the blocks."

Wilbur and I read the newly published work of Caleb Gattegno, on the use of the Cuisenaire Rods. Wilbur created worksheets to complement the rods and help with understanding computational skills.

By building with the calibrated unit blocks in the wood room, children gained familiarity with their size, proportion, and weight. They had to estimate and calculate how to balance them to engineer stable structures. With table blocks and plastic shapes, they built three-dimensional geometric constructions and drew two-dimensional shapes with rulers and compasses.

Wilbur created geo-boards and shape boards with worksheets for exploring geometric shapes and understanding concepts, such as area, perimeter, division, and fractions. We also used conventional math workbooks in which math problems were presented sequentially. With these, the children could work independently, counting with their fingers as well as using structural materials, such as an abacus, buttons, and ice cream sticks.

Reading, Writing and Mathematics

As with the reading program, we expected that the combination of formal and informal learning experiences would provide the structures required for learning mathematical concepts. We had not yet heard of the Nuffield Math book series (published in 1967) or the theories of Constance Kamii, with their ideas for helping children develop their mathematical curiosity from their own experiences. These would have been of great assistance formulating the math program. Chapter seven describes how we implemented the skills program over four years and the results we achieved.

Working with geo boards and
shape boards.

Reading, Writing and Mathematics

Calculating with *Cuisenaire Rods.*

Voices of Children

Constructing with table blocks
and plastic shapes.

Reading, Writing and Mathematics

New studies of 'active learning' show that when children play with toys they are acting a lot like scientists doing experiments.

– Alison Gopnik

Science, like art, is not a copy of nature but a re-creation of her . . .
We re-make nature by the act of discovery,
in the poem or in the theorem.
And the great poem and the deep theorem
are new to every reader,
and yet are his own experience,
because he himself re-creates them.

– Jacob Bronowski

Chapter 5

Science: Children's Discoveries

While children interpret their world through their own symbol making in the arts, they are also working to discover how their world works and how they can act upon it to obtain desired outcomes. Alison Gopnik and Andrew Meltzoff have studied this process, as well as brain development. They theorize that children form successive theories about how their world functions. To arrive at their theories, children observe, ask questions, conduct trials, make predictions, hypothesize, and draw conclusions. They employ the same cognitive structures as scientists to research and develop their theories.

At the time of our school, we were inspired by the writings of the scientist/educator David Hawkins, whose thinking prefigured the ideas developed by Gopnik and Meltzer. Of special interest was Hawkins' article "Messing About in Science" (1965), in which he propounded his philosophy of learning in the context of science education. Hawkins developed his ideas while working at the Massachusetts Institute of Technology on developing an elementary school science program. It was sponsored by the National Science Foundation as a response to the Russians' launch of the space probe *Sputnik* (1957) and the concern it generated in the United States about our ability to compete globally in math and science. Working together, scientists and science teachers created the Elementary Science Study Program (ESS). The (ESS) units are designed to encourage teachers and children to experiment with familiar objects to demonstrate scientific concepts. Working in their own ways, participants can define questions, set goals, and make their own discoveries. By keeping and sharing records of their findings, students can create resources for further exploration.

Hawkins' thoughts about education stemmed from his observations of college students, who often seemed to lack a basic grasp of abstract concepts in science. He also observed young people experimenting and exploring in school settings and came to believe that children's abilities to theorize and think abstractly derived from extended experience with the concrete workings of underlying phenomena. He thought that children should have substantial time to probe and experiment with materials on their own, without instruction or superimposed questions from adults.

He wrote, "This is not all there is to learning, of course; but it is the magical part, and the part most often killed in school."

Hawkins concluded that children's active involvement and their method of trial and error would create the frame of mind to raise questions, hypothesize, test, reach conclusions, and develop generalizations and abstractions. The teachers' role would be to observe the children's activities and help them find connections as they developed their own pathways to knowledge. Half a century ago, Hawkins' theories about how children learn corroborated our thoughts about the importance of children's play and self-directed activities.

Creating a Science Program

At our school, we sought to create an environment with natural and man-made science-related materials and ideas to inspire the children to make their own discoveries and develop theories about their world. We used several of the ESS units, including Batteries and Bulbs and Kitchen Physics. With the Batteries and Bulbs unit, the teachers demonstrated how to connect circuits with batteries and light up bulbs, while observing the behavior of electricity in the process. Children learned how to do this and were able to experiment on their own. We discussed the power of electricity and some of its functions, as well as different sources of power: animal and human labor, steam, wind, water, air, gas, and the machines they powered.

With the ESS Kitchen Physics unit, we used common substances to observe physical and chemical properties. We started by mixing baking soda and vinegar and watched them explode into a mass of fulminating bubbles. When the kids were able to do this on their own, we helped them build a "volcano" from sawdust and paste, into

Mixing baking soda and vinegar for
science experiment on the roof.

Science: Children's Discoveries

which they inserted the potent mixture to simulate a volcanic eruption. At other times, we tied the four ends of a square of cloth with string and placed it over the mixture as it exploded and propelled the parachute into the air. We did not delve into the causality of this phenomenon. It would be a topic for future studies in chemistry.

The Children's Kitchen Physics Lab

These and other experiences, combined with the urge that led scientists and alchemists to find out how things work, inspired some of the children to develop their own Kitchen Physics experiments. It started with a couple of children mixing on their own and asking for more supplies. Gradually, more children were attracted to the activity and set up their "lab" in a little-used small room equipped with tables and chairs. We helped them collect the equipment they needed: containers, plates, pans, spoons, jar tops, and tongue depressors. They gathered flour, salt, sugar, baking soda, sawdust, soap, Ajax, vinegar, and vegetable coloring for mixing their experiments. The kids mixed these ingredients in various proportions and sometimes added water. They saved samples of their mixtures on trays, jar tops and bottles and were eager to see what changes took place over time. Articulating and sharing their observations were part of the process.

For example:

"Look, this one is hard and turned brown."

"This one's still soft."

"This one got all crumbly."

They used the scientist's method of trial and error.

Someone called these mixtures "formulas," and the kids grasped the concept that a formula can yield predictable results. By repeating and varying the formulas, they observed what combinations produced what results. They hypothesized: "What will happen if we use less flour and more salt?" or more water, etc. "Let's check the formulas," as they examined them throughout the day.

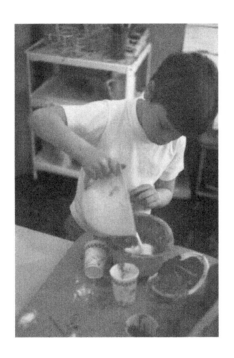

Mixing "formulas."

The children had created their own library, newspaper, broadcast stations, and museums, and now set up their own "lab" in which to conduct their experiments. We, the teachers, assisted by providing supplies and consultations, and by observing what took place. Over our years of teaching, we had observed children exploring materials, but we had not seen such sustained activity by school-age children working independently.

Wilbur's only saved record of the Kitchen Physics Lab depicts some of the wild flights of imagination that children entertain as part of the process of discovery and making connections:

◄ I pull from my collection of school records a note on Alex and Michael, who at the moment of my observation are engaged in "Kitchen Physics," mixing common household products: soap powder, cleanser, baking soda, vinegar, vegetable coloring.

Alex: Do you think this formula will really make a martini? Listen, here's a new one. I made it up myself, but don't put my name on it. It's a new experiment. I put in a few drops of acid, then a few drops of sawdust. Then we sit around for a while. Then we get a snail and dump that in. And we find some scoops of ice cream and dump them in. It's delicious! Boy, is this going to be a good joke on Eric, ain't it?

Michael: Yeah! I'll buy some real ice cream to put in it!

Alex's' eyes dilate as he looks at Michael with an air of incredulity.

Alex: Nah! Don't you get it? This is supposed to be a joke."

►

Alex had certainly been around adult cocktail hours and noted that martinis are the result of mixtures. In the lab he had the power to go beyond a given formula and, in his mind, improvised his concoction. Immediately, he grasped that this was an absurd idea not to be put into action. Alex's mind functioned like a scientist's in the sense of imagining or constructing novel combinations, not knowing whether they would be used or discarded. He also mixed reality with flights of fancy, somewhat like the mad scientist or a science fiction character engaged in fantasy and having fun with jokes.

Michael was not aware of this process and surprised Alex as he interpreted the "joke" literally and wanted to make it happen. Alex was concerned and told him: "Nah! Don't you get it? This is supposed to be a joke." This was an idea to ignore and it remained so.

One day, Mark gave us a fright by announcing that he had tasted some of his formula. We rushed him to a doctor who found him to be unharmed. Mark then said that he had pretended to taste it. It did not matter: the idea that someone might imbibe these ingredients made us concerned about the safety of this activity. Were we too confident in the ability of six- and seven-year-olds to distinguish what was safe to eat? Could this happen in a situation where children were more supervised? Was this Mark's idea of a joke? After discussions with the staff and with the children about the dangers of swallowing substances like Ajax, we decided to allow the Kitchen Physics Lab to continue. The scientists met, mixed, and experimented for many weeks until they moved on to other pursuits.

The children were curious to handle, observe, and test the materials and forces that shape their physical environment. From these experiences, they raised questions, hypothesized, and developed theories.

In his article, "Messing About in Science," David Hawkins recommends following up on the children's play and independent inquiries with keeping records of their discoveries. He calls for discussion and research to lead the children to develop their abilities to theorize and think abstractly.

At the Fifteenth Street School, we expanded the children's activities through discussions and research. I remember that we made notations of the Kitchen Physics Lab and other experiences but did not save them. It would have been useful to have a card index with records of the children's experiments and their theories about them. These could have been added to the science books in the class library, and we could have used them for further discussions and research.

We also used the New York City Public School Curriculum guides. We focused on studies of technology and mechanics, magnetism, weather, heat/fire, space and astronomy, and plants and animals.

Science: Children's Discoveries

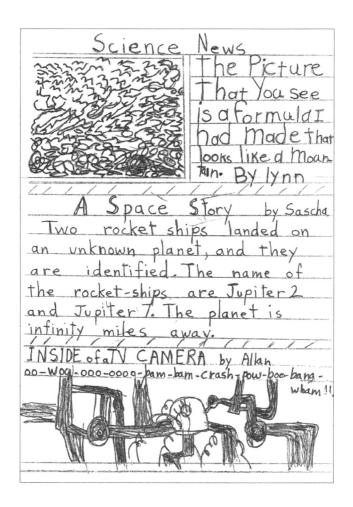

Science News.

Formula left to dry and observe.

Technology and Mechanics

At the time, computers were just coming into popular use but were not included in the school. Wilbur worked with the children to create simple machines. They experimented with balance toys, levers, gravity chutes, and pendulums. They also made their own inventions by disassembling and recombining discarded machine parts and electronic chips. From these they created steering wheels for cars and space ships, and their versions of radios and TV sets for their broadcasts. Sara discovered she could make concentric circles by pressing a magic marker over a paper rotating on a turntable. That's when *machine art* was born in our classroom.

The children explored the mysterious, examining the workings of junked TV sets, radio innards, the jointings, and the connections. Some children learned to connect circuits and light bulbs on their own and used them in their block buildings and carpentry projects. They constructed pulleys, and Chris discovered how to play a record by pressing a piece of wire on a revolving disc at 33 rpm.

We looked at books about mechanics and examined and discussed locomotion engines and household appliances and the forces that propel them.

Magnetism

We brought magnets of various sizes and tested what they attracted and repelled. We also found a grinding machine with which the kids made filings from nails and other metal objects. By moving a magnet under filings scattered over a piece of paper, the children created patterns as the bits drew together into aggregate forms. "Watch the magic metal walk across the paper," someone commented, as he demonstrated these properties to fellow students and visitors. We looked at books to learn more about the nature of magnetism and how it relates to the earth.

Examining the inside of a TV set.

Exploring fire with Rachel.

Voices of Children

Weather, Heat, and Fire

Some students developed an interest in the weather and the changes that affected it, such as cloud formation and the seasons. When we brought in a hygrometer that collected and measured rainfall and moved in the direction of the wind, the kids decided to set up a weather station on the deck.

They began to monitor the station and issued frequent weather reports, which were communicated to the group through impromptu "broadcasts" from "radio" and "TV stations."

"This is station WEAT, your weather channel. Today, we are expecting clouds, and a northwest wind is bringing cool breezes."

Some of the reports were based on observations and others came from imagination. The weather station continued to operate through the spring to the end of that school year.

While on the deck, some children had learned how to direct the sun's rays with a magnifying glass and discovered how to burn a hole through paper and to melt crayons. We experimented with how various substances responded to heat and fire. The children wondered and discussed why some burned more easily than others, e.g. steel wool versus string.

Outer Space and Astronomy

During the mid-sixties, when the NASA program was being developed, teachers and children at our school watched early launches on the television set in the secretary's office. We had never seen anything like these helmeted, silver-suited astronauts, in capsules launched into space by fiery blasts.

After each launch, we anticipated seeing how the NASA ground team guided the space capsule as it reentered the earth's atmosphere and parachuted to its splashdown in the ocean. We cheered when the astronauts emerged and were lifted to safety on a ship or helicop-

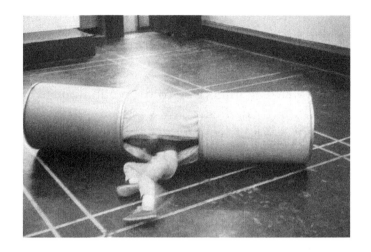

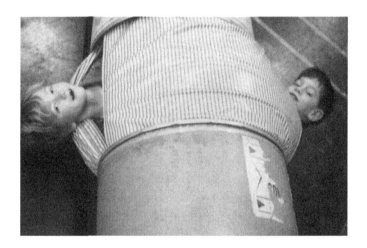

top & bottom: The "space capsule"
in the gym.

ter. In our minds, we were with these explorers venturing to where no one had traveled before to discover the nature of the universe. We knew we were witnessing history in the making.

Children had long used space and spacemen as topics in their play. They had heard of imagined Martian invasions and seen the "Buck Rogers in the 25th Century" popular comic strip, with its stories about travels to distant planets. As these subjects were rooted in the realm of fantasy, teachers had generally regarded them as inappropriate for school. Now, flesh-and-blood astronauts made voyages in real crafts and used modern technology to navigate into the beyond. Fantasy had become reality, and in many schools, teachers and students watched the space program unfold on their television sets.

At our school, the children's minds were stimulated by the space explorations they had seen on TV, and they took roles in scenarios they created about these events. In the gym, Chris and David simulated space capsules by combining the cylindrical cardboard containers and foam pads. They squeezed inside, and with their body movements, rolled the capsule around the gym floor. When their "space trip" was completed, they waved to their fans as they emerged from their ship. And girls and boys worked out space maneuvers by attaching long ribbons to coat racks to simulate walks in space, the first of which had recently been aired on TV.

In the Wood Room, children created their version of a space station. Several boys built a space ship with the large and small building blocks. They spent much time remodeling it and building new models. From the platform on a side wall, they enacted countdowns, launches, and return landings. We helped them make space suits from Saran Wrap and found old machine parts for instrument panels and navigational tools, as well as books on astronomy. Boys and girls made murals and a three-dimensional paper mache model of the solar system, which they displayed in their space station.

Louis created a space vehicle from blocks and small electronic components from our surplus store collection. He asked Wilbur to help him move the recorder near his elaborate construction so he could record the ship's journey.

Louis: "Hello Ladies and Gentlemen from station WKET. This morning, we are reporting from Cape Canaveral and take you inside the space capsule. Okay, here is the motor and the fuel tank to take us into space at the signal of NASA, and this is the section for storing the recording equipment for when we get to the moon."

Louis points to a bottle cap mounted on a panel.

"When we press this button, the door will open automatically, and the camera will move to where I direct it."

"What do you hope to discover on the moon?" Wilbur asked.

"We want to know if there's water, and if there are living things there. Of course, we also have equipment to take samples of rocks and what we find there."

"And what are these plastic pieces over there?"

"These are our space suits, which Billy and I will wear when we are ready to get out."

"I see," Wilbur said. "Will you be able to walk? Do you think you will have gravity there?"

Pointing to the innards of an old TV set, Louis responded.

"Yeah, we worked on it. We have special gravity attractors."

Louis was the main spaceship operator and was not fazed. At that moment, he was improvising the existence of "gravity attractors" to solve the problem. He both grasped and imagined the mechanics and science involved in space exploration. Louis was planning for the future, as the first moon landing occurred several years later.

Some students took active roles in these projects, and some came by to check, discuss the events, ask questions, and make suggestions.

As part of the children's imaginary space-related scenarios, the guinea pigs, once more, became characters in dramas and took on the role of astronauts. When the astronauts Scott Carpenter and John Glenn were honored with parades in New York City, the kids decided to honor their own guinea pig astronaut with a celebration. We helped them gather the materials they wanted: flags, homemade signs, banners and streamers, and small musical instruments. Many participated in the preparations, and everyone was invited to join in. The parade proceeded to the beat of drums and tambourines as the child astronauts, holding Guinea Pig astronaut, began their walk through the third-floor rooms and down the stairs. Moving solemnly through the building, they gathered about twenty participants. I joined at the rear while Wilbur took photos. We marched slowly

Drawing of moon shot projected for
1971 (actual date c 1967).

Science: Children's Discoveries

around the gym to the podium. Held aloft for all to see, the guinea pig blinked his eyes as someone proclaimed him "the first guinea pig to land on the moon."

When interviewed for one of the children's radio stations, the guinea pig was asked, "Did you find water on the moon?" "He says no," as someone interpreted the squeaking sounds he made in response to being stroked. The animals were treated with love and respect. The festivities over, the children returned upstairs and posed for a photo in front of the block spaceship with the guinea pig astronaut and his reward: a large carrot.

This was an impromptu event: imagined, organized, and executed within one morning. It is impossible to describe the sense of joy and involvement visible in the children's expressions and body language as they prepared and carried out their parade. It was a high point of their space exploration. Beginning with current events, the children absorbed and interpreted historic and scientific information and reconstructed it into their own dramatic creation. It required the exercise of their creative, imaginative, and cognitive faculties. In view of the complex teamwork involved, it is noteworthy that no one was in charge of the project. I don't know who came up with the idea and enrolled others in the enterprise. Someone asked for drums and tambourines, and others for flags and red, white, and blue streamers. I don't know who planned the return of Guinea Pig astronaut to his/ her spaceship or where the carrot came from. It evolved without a previous design. We supported the children's plans and worked to foster and expand their ideas by supplying books, materials, constructive conversation, and, of course, appreciation.

Whether in or out of school, children spontaneously create and enact scenarios about significant life events. In this instance, the availability of space, time, and support from the environment allowed this expression to develop to its full potential as a learning exercise and as a personal experience.

Wilbur recorded some of the children's "space" conversations in the Wood Room. These accurately demonstrate the children's grasp of some of the complexities involved in space operations, such as the hazards and moment-by-moment decisions facing the NASA teams. They understood the use of specific terms to denote operations and

Parade in Gym for "First guinea pig
to land on the moon."

"Astronauts" and their block
space capsule.

Science: Children's Discoveries

how they can be fraught with difficulties. The children carefully noted the details of actual space flights they witnessed on their television screens at home or at school. Takeoffs were sometimes delayed and unfulfilled, as in the first United States attempt to lock separate space vehicles while in orbit.

These two unedited transcripts are from recordings of children's conversations we had on tape for the library.

Sean, John, and Sasha (all seven-year-olds) are playing "space." John, the "control" on the NASA ground team, fiddles with an old non-functioning radio to communicate with the two "astronauts" who have ventured out into space on a play platform in the classroom.

Control (to Astronauts): Are you all right up there?

Astronauts: Yes, we made repairs. I've got some of the greatest shots of the sun you ever saw.

Control: Don't get too close to the sun because I heard it is too hot there. If your scooters blow up, you'll be stuck there forever. Our rescue missiles are not launched yet.

Astronaut 1: We are on a normal gravity planet.

Astronaut 2: And normal air.

Control: The chief says next thing to do is land on the moon. Some people say there are creatures, so be careful. Over and out.

Astronaut 1: I see a creature!

Control: Stop the report! Destroy him!

(Sound of shooting)

Astronaut 1: Our laser beams seemed to have worked!

Control: You are running low on fuel. Try for re-entry.

Issues of life, death, violence, and the unknown have always concerned children and been part of their play, though the ease with which life is eliminated raises questions about presentations seen on TV. In other conversations, some kids imagine that they would encounter monsters and robots on other planets (as seen on the TV show "Space Patrol"). In this episode, the children have demonstrated their awareness of the teamwork in the spaceship and on the ground and how they needed to be coordinated.

Wilbur wrote about another scenario involving guinea pigs and a moon landing:

◄ Billy, aged seven, was vitally interested in space travel. To him it was no fantasy, but a human operation about which he could learn and comment upon. One time he asked me to introduce a broadcast. The record of Billy's words is unedited.

"Ladies and gentlemen," I began, "this is 1967 at Cape Canaveral, and we are ready for the guinea pigs' flight. I now switch you over to the control room where Billy will report on the action."

"We seem to have some difficulty in Computer 2," said Billy. "This computer will show the guineas how they will land. They will land in a rocket ship 15 stories high. This test is to see if the guineas can live on the moon's atmosphere. They will go from Earth past the moon's atmosphere and return to Earth. Due to trouble in Computer 2, we delay the flight for two hours until 6:00 p.m. Signing off until 6:00 p.m."

Billy paused and continued:

"Good evening, ladies and gentlemen. This is from Cape Canaveral, June 6, where we had the problem earlier on Computer 2, but we seem to fix it and we are ready for the flight. The countdown is about to start. 10-9-8-7-6-5-4-3-2-1-0, ignition and fire! (Sound effects) It looks like a good blast-off for the guinea pigs. (More sound effects) They are a thousand feet high. The first stage went off five seconds ago. They are getting past Earth's atmosphere—they also have a movie in the guineas' compartment. They have everything: food, water. (Sound effects) Second stage went off and they are heading for the moon's atmosphere. There is a little difficulty with the radars. The radars are fixed. I am pleased to be able to report that the re-entry was successful. As we have reported, the astronauts were properly honored with a parade."

The use of the word "report" in the last recording is of particular interest. It seems apparent that the children of this age understand and use the term appropriately. This means that they have moved far beyond the range of egocentricism into a social world of articulation and representation about social events in the world. The image of the astronaut is par-

Science: Children's Discoveries

The beauty of plants and flowers inspires
wonder and joy, and by caring for them,
we participate in the miracle of creation.

Voices of Children

ticularly compelling for young children, which is why they use it in their play.

The study of space flight is not earthbound, it allows for the expression of the organic love of freedom, freedom from weight and gravity that is experienced in moments of joy and excitement, moments in which hope floods our organism, and we reaffirm our faith in tackling the impossible. The very words "fantasy" and "reality" are misleading. The children's play, as creation that incorporates both, transcends them. ➤

Using their imaginations to simulate space exploration, the children created constructs through which they could enact and absorb the components of what they have observed, read, and discussed about the subject. They incorporated the mechanics, sequences, and language employed by the NASA teams they have seen on TV broadcasts and we discussed in school.

Undergirding the technicalities of space travel and discovery is a sense of awe at the world beyond our earth. From their classroom on Fifteenth Street, the children's imaginations reached out to experience and comprehend the mysteries of the universe.

Albert Einstein wrote: "Imagination is more important than knowledge. Knowledge is limited; imagination encircles the world."

Learning About Nature: Biophilia

From the time Edward O. Wilson was a boy, he was fascinated with ants, and his lifelong study of them led him to develop his theories of biodiversity.

In his book *Biophilia* (1984), he explores the connection between humans and the living universe. He defines biophilia as "the innate tendency to focus on life and lifelike processes" as "a deep and complicated process in mental development." When given opportunities, children develop their interest in relating to and learning about the animals and plants that share their environment.

Though our school was located in an urban environment, it was important to connect with the world of nature, with its plants, animals, sky, earth, water, and weather. On our trips to parks and the river, we observed and enjoyed the sparrows, pigeons, robins, butterflies, squirrels, trees, and flowers, and the constant wonder of the natural phenomena all around us. To our classroom, we brought plants and animals, bones, stones, shells, and abandoned birds' and wasps' nests for study and enjoyment. In the following section, I write about how the children interacted with plants and animals in our school.

To our classroom, we brought fruits and vegetables that we cut and examined with the children. They ate the edible parts and planted the seeds and pits. We found willow and other branches that we placed in jars with water and watched their roots and leaves emerge. We measured their growth and made graphs. The children liked to sprout beans in a see-through cup between a wet paper towel and observe the development of their roots, stems, and leaves. With flowers and their plantings, the children created imaginative "installations" by arranging them in boxes with objects such as pinecones, leaves and twigs, dried flowers, and plastic figures.

A Farm Grows in Manhattan

On one of our field trips, we visited the Botanical Garden and studied the varieties of plants and the environments that produced them. On a visit to Central Park, I noticed brown piles of mashed-up leaves mixed with mud.

"Look, these leaves are breaking down; let's take some to school and see what happens to them," I said.

We scooped some of the mixture into plastic bags, and in school, moved it into cups and cans. Every day, the kids stirred it, added water, and chopped it into finer pieces. It was an approximation of the mulch/soil-making process. We read about the formation of soil and the role of worms and microorganisms and talked about the seasons and the cycle of growth and decay. For the class library, we brought books on nature and botany as well as stories, such as *The Carrot Seed* and *Jack and the Beanstalk*.

Voices of Children

Plant environment in
a drawer.

At the Botanical Garden.

Science: Children's Discoveries

A group of six kids aged six to eight became fascinated with these horticultural activities. They used soil and some of the mulch we collected in the park to make plantings in plastic and paper cups. To hold these, Wilbur brought two empty drawers that he placed on tables in the Art Room.

The boys and girls gathered regularly to water their plants, compare sizes and number of leaves, add new plants, and share ideas. They made drawings and wrote about them, and we helped them with measuring and graphing the growing stems.

They named this conglomerate "The Farm of the Six."

The Farm captured the children's imagination, and Danny T, his blue eyes flashing with enthusiasm, told the group: "When we finish school, we'll all live on the farm and have jobs."

In their minds, the Farm existed in the present and the future simultaneously. They imagined living together in a metaphoric communal society they created.

"We'll grow things and have animals."

"We'll need to buy stuff like shovels, pitchforks, and machines."

John pointed to the decomposing leaves.

"Let's try to get money for our farm and sell our soil in the park," he said.

"Who will you sell to?" Wilbur asked.

"Just people we see."

We found small bags for them, and on our next visit to our local park, they approached a man on a bench with their offer: 25 cents for a bag of soil. Wilbur and I chuckled silently as we watched the kids in their first business enterprise. At the same time, we were concerned with what might come from encounters with strangers. We stood by and watched the event take its course. Though people were intrigued with the children's story, the kids made only a couple of sales. They gave up but continued planning for the future:

"And we'll need buildings for ourselves and the animals."

"When I was in Vermont, I saw cows and barns."

"Cows! Cows have babies. What will we do when our cows have babies and there are too many cows?"

"Farmers sell their cows, and they are killed, and butchers sell their meat."

Voices of Children

Rules for the Farm

These are things people should try to do:
1. Not to discuss blood and death.
2. Not to lie.
3. Remember—you only get 100 more chances.
4. No meaness
5. Try not to fight.
6. If you do any of these things you lose a chance.
7. Just share everything including money.
8. Build don't sell.

FARM OF THE 6.

Rules for the Farm.

"I wouldn't want our cows to be killed."

"No, No."

Everyone agreed.

Over the next few days they met and talked about finding ways to deal with the cow problem.

Wilbur recorded some of their thoughts in a meeting they set up to find a solution and to think about how to run the farm.

"Everyone on the farm gets one hundred chances."

"Yeah, and you shouldn't be mean or fight."

"And you shouldn't lie."

"And if you do these things, you lose one chance."

"Yeah, but what about the cows and their babies?"

Out of the silence a soft voice piped up. "Barns! We'll build more barns and they can all live in the barns!" said Lisa.

All eyes opened wide and a collective smile spread over the group.

"Yes, barns, we'll build more barns."

"We won't sell the cows. And don't talk about blood and death."

"And we'll share everything, money too."

Wilbur and the "six" schematized their ideas in a document that was printed and distributed to the entire class.

Wilbur summed this up as follows:

◄ This is the kind of expression, truly child-like, that Rachel and I like to think typified the situation. The rules are naively expressed, direct, sincere, generous:

"Remember, you only get 100 more chances."

It is apparent that the children are striving to arrive at rational social behavior derived from their school-related work.

►

After their meeting, the "six" continued tending their gardens and sharing ideas till they went on to follow other interests.

On The Farm, the children had imbued commonplace objects with their own meanings. They enacted their interpretation of the role of farmers but were not aware that they also functioned as planners, entrepreneurs, legislators, and philosophers. Eventually, The Farm vanished, and I want to believe that the children's creativity and capacity for bonding and solving problems with their peers remained active and grew in their future lives. Seeds....

Voices of Children

I am not able to analyze the particular web of connections that created the atmosphere for these events to unfold. The children's own motivation, curiosity, and wonder led them to construct the concept of The Farm of the Six and to work together on a format for governance. As teachers, we set the stage, assisted, encouraged the children's creative process, and shared the excitement as their expressions took form. The Farm of the Six and its social contract laid a framework for understanding the concept of ecology and the interdependence of living things, as well as the foundation for the rule of law. As these threads of learning merge, science, philosophy, and social studies blend into an integrated, synergetic unit.

Since that time, a number of schools have developed gardening programs, such as the "Edible Playground," featuring the growing and preparation of food, and related studies in environmental issues, as well as experiences in learning basic skills. Perhaps, somewhere, there exists another Farm of the Six.

Animals in Our Classroom

The children enjoyed and learned from the various animals that visited or lived at the school. These included guinea pigs, Bunny Wunny, frogs, and others.

When we brought two guinea pigs to our classroom, the kids named them Florence and Peter. While helping Wilbur feed them and clean their tank, Celia noticed that Peter was getting fat. Wilbur checked and realized that Peter was pregnant.

"Looks like we're going to have baby guinea pigs here soon," Wilbur told Celia.

Word spread, and excited children gathered round the tank to look at and pet the mother to be. At this age, the children knew that males don't have babies, and they changed Peter's name to Florence and vice versa.

Naturally, kids had questions about the animals' anatomy and reproduction. As Wilbur and I had not been around guinea pigs, these questions were new to us, and we turned to books to learn that

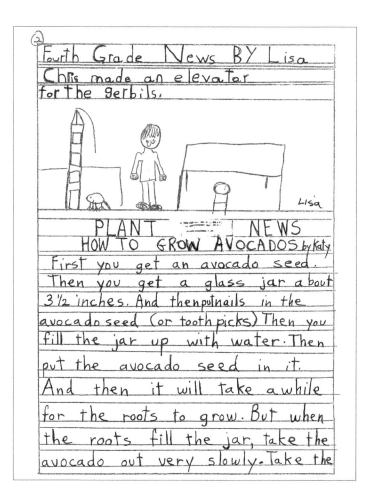

Fourth Grade News BY Lisa
Chris made an elevator
for the gerbils.

Lisa

PLANT NEWS
HOW TO GROW AVOCADOS by Katy
First you get an avocado seed.
Then you get a glass jar about
3½ inches. And then put nails in the
avocado seed (or toothpicks) Then you
fill the jar up with water. Then
put the avocado seed in it.
And then it will take a while
for the roots to grow. But when
the roots fill the jar, take the
avocado out very slowly. Take the

left & right: How to grow avocados.

③ nails out and put the seed
into a flower pot. Add dirt so
that the avocado is halfway
covered. Then water it, and
water it every few days.
Put it in the sun. The End

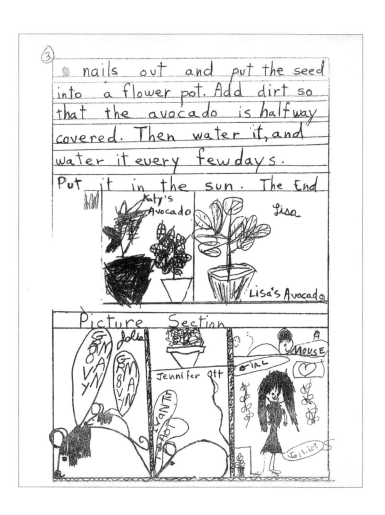

Katy's Avocado

Lisa

Lisa's Avocado

Picture Section

Jennifer Ott

MOUSE

GIRL

Bunny Wunny visits Museum of
Natural Guinea Pig History.

we could expect three or four pups in approximately eight weeks. Everyone was curious about distinguishing boy from girl guinea pigs and wanted to examine their bodies. Holding a squirming guinea pig upside down and looking for what was hiding under thick folds of fur was no easy matter, and after a time, we gave up trying. We found illustrations and photos in books.

When the birthing time approached, Billy became concerned and asked, "How do they do it? With doctors?" Before I could think of an explanation, Seth replied, "Animals know how. My cat had kittens just like Florence. She licked them clean." Billy looked pensive as he gazed at a distant spot. "Dr. Guinea, can't you see it chewed in letters on a leaf—Dr. Guinea, MD." Seth and Billy had come up with their own logical questions and responses, and Billy's imagination took flight. After the birth:

George: "Hey, come see the new guinea pigs!"

Jim: "They're so big, they don't look newborn at all."

George: "Yeah, they don't grow by years—they grow by months. I guess mice don't even grow by months, they're so small, I bet they grow by days."

George had created his own theory of how growth periods might match up with the life cycles of different animals. He observed, speculated, imagined, and hypothesized. Without being aware of it, George had formulated his own version of relativity: time is the same everywhere, though it manifests in different frames. The children's questions and observations were part of the larger ongoing dialogue between children, with each other and their teachers.

After several guinea pig litters were born, another four-footed, furry friend joined our class; he was a large white rabbit that someone loaned to the school, and the kids named Bunny Wunny. During the day, he roamed freely, was petted and fed, visited the block constructions, the Museum of Natural Guinea Pig History, and hung around during reading sessions. At night Bunny Wunny stayed in a cage. During his tenure, one of the guinea pigs gave birth to a litter that, for the first time, included a white guinea pig.

"Do you think Bunny Wunny got out of his cage and brought us the white Guinea Pig?" someone asked. The answer came from the imagination of an unknown author who dictated the following story

Science: Children's Discoveries

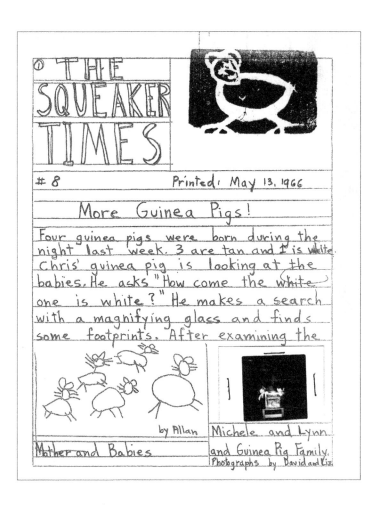

① THE SQUEAKER TIMES

#8   Printed: May 13, 1966

More Guinea Pigs!

Four guinea pigs were born during the night last week. 3 are tan and 1 is white. Chris' guinea pig is looking at the babies. He asks "How come the white one is white?" He makes a search with a magnifying glass and finds some footprints. After examining the

by Allan

Mother and Babies

Michele and Lynn and Guinea Pig Family. Photographs by David and Liz

left & right: The Squeaker Times story,
"More Guinea Pigs."

Voices of Children

footprints he says: "I think Bunny-
Wunny brought that guinea to us
while we were sleeping."
David's guinea pig says:
"I think Bunny-Wunny brought us
the white guinea because he
liked us so much. I found Bunny-
Wunny's footprints, I checked his
prints in my file."

Animal Bones Examined 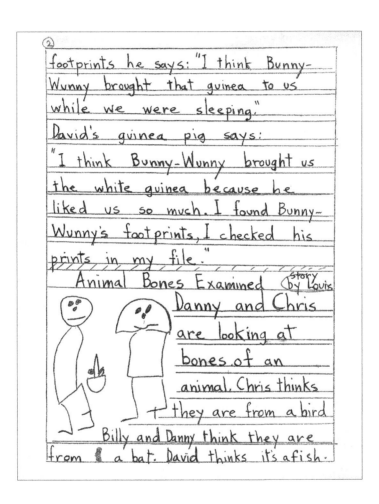 story
by Louis

Danny and Chris
are looking at
bones of an
animal. Chris thinks
they are from a bird
Billy and Danny think they are
from a bat. David thinks it's a fish.

to me. It was published in *The Squeaker Times*, with drawings and photos made by Allan, Lynn, and David.

Four guinea pigs were born during the night last week. Three are tan and one is white. Chris's guinea pig asks, *"How come the white one is white?"* He makes a search with a magnifying glass and finds some footprints. After examining the footprints, he says, *"I think Bunny Wunny brought that guinea pig to us while we were sleeping."*

David's guinea pig says: *"I think Bunny Wunny brought us the white guinea pig because he liked us so much. I found Bunny Wunny's footprints in my file."*

Once more, the children assigned imaginary roles to the guinea pigs, this time as detectives, complete with their own "footprint file."

Bunny Wunny eventually returned to his home, while Florence and Peter's offspring continued to perpetuate themselves, to the on-going delight of the children. The children's families, as well as friends of the school, adopted some of the guinea pig babies. Bill Schenker remembers taking his favorite, Peter Munchkin, with him when he moved to California, and recalls the funeral when the guinea pig died and was buried near Bill's home. Inevitably, a guinea pig died at school, and we were able to bury it in someone's yard. Most everyone remembered losing a cat, dog, or grandparent, and much as we talked and read about death, it remained, as ever, incomprehensible.

The presence of the animals generated many questions about the unknown: of anatomy, gender, procreation, and the children's own bodies. We did not develop a formal program to address these questions, but dealt with them informally as they arose.

More Animal Visitors

In the spring, Wilbur and I found frog egg masses in country ponds and brought them to a terrarium Wilbur built for them. We all watched the tiny tadpoles swim free of their jelly pouches and, over weeks, metamorphose into froglets with legs and enlarged heads. They climbed onto the mossy bank of their tank, and when they were ready to be on their own, we took them to Central Park. The kids worried as the frogs hopped into a pond. "Will they find food?" "Will snakes eat them?" Dialogue, books, and research brought answers and more questions. With today's broader understanding of ecology, I'm not sure that letting the frogs go in Central Park was the right thing to do, but it was a fascinating experience.

Wilbur went into further detail:

◄ Frog eggs brought from a pond in Croton were transformed, not into fantasy princes, but actual frogs who lived contented in the terrarium I built with swimming pool and forest plants: ferns, British redcoat, rattlesnake plantain, and a shelf fungus from a broken oak tree limb.

"Now the frogs won't be lonely," someone said, as into the terrarium went earthworms, these fascinating denizens of below the surface. They were joined by green newts and red efts: aquatic dwellers we collected and returned to their muddy woodlands when they turned into salamanders. David and Chris specialized in providing food (consisting of mealy worms procured at a pet shop) and water for the terrarium. ►

We also brought caterpillars and snails into our classroom. We created appropriate homes for them where the children fed and observed them. A child remarked: "We found caterpillars in the spring. Mine likes leaves. You know they aren't always this way. They turn into butterflies and things."

We purchased chicken eggs in an incubator. After they hatched, we cared for the chicks until they were ready to be taken to a farm.

To learn more about the various animals, the children could find information in the science books in the class library. They could also read tales about fantasy characters such as Curious George, Stuart Little, and Bambi, animals with human emotions and behaviors, metaphors for human experience. Books in the class library included the *Frog and Toad* series, *The Very Hungry Caterpillar, Danny the Dinosaur, Millions of Cats, Curious George, Harry the Dirty Dog, Black Beauty, Bambi, Charlotte's Web, Stuart Little, Aesop's Fables* and the

Science: Children's Discoveries

Brer Rabbit stories. In turn, the children were inspired to create their own animal characters in imaginative stories and scenarios, writings, and drawings.

Animals are also depicted in music. Wilbur played his guitar and taught songs, such as "Fox Went Out on a Starry Night," "Molly Hare," "Froggy Went a'Courtin'," "Blue Oh Blue," "Bluebird Flying in my Window," and "John the Rabbit." By observing, discussing, and interpreting through the arts, the children enriched their understanding about the phenomena of their world.

Besides the sheer love and pleasure the children experienced in the company of their animal friends, they learned to care for, observe, and appreciate the diversity of living creatures who shared their world. We hoped that their school experiences would provide the scaffolding for developing the knowledge and empathy needed to sustain their changing planet.

Wilbur observed these relationships:

◄ The creatures of the world are for children an endless source of interest, delight and sympathetic relationships. Children respond to their movements and spontaneity, their warmth and responsiveness, their vulnerability, their independence, their quiet confidence in managing their affairs. And the children relate to the similarities the animals bear to the featherless, furless, scale-less humanoids, as well as to their differences.

From tiny mouse to guinea pig, from snake to armored turtle, animals form a boundless source of observation, speculation, and affinity, and offer a deep abiding relationship. They are another phenomenon that connects the child with the vast web of existence.

And, above all else, the children relate to the warm, quivering heartbeat of creature guinea. They relate to the mute creatures who reveal their dispositions and pleasure at being gently held in the presence of the larger, quivering warmth of the creatures we call children. ►

Animals from the Past and Evolution

The children learned from plants and animals in our present world, and some children took an interest in what the world was like in the past. In our history studies, the children were able to imagine the past in an earlier America; now they imagined a very distant time when the earth was inhabited by dinosaurs.

Some of the children had visited the Museum of Natural History with their parents and took an interest in dinosaurs and their history. They brought plastic replicas to school and created environments for them. We followed up with finding materials for study, such as maps showing bone deposits in Montana. We read passages from the geologist/explorer John Wesley Powell's book *The Exploration of the Colorado River and its Canyon,* in which he describes his discovery of fossils of early sea creatures in the rock formations along the Colorado River in 1869.

We took a class trip to the Museum of Natural History. "How many million years old is this?" "How long ago were the dinosaurs on earth?" the kids wondered. We thought, discussed, and researched the distant past and evolution.

Inspired by the dioramas at the museum, some of the boys created special environments for their toy dinosaurs in a small sandbox Wilbur made for the Wood Room. They piled sand into mounds for the dinosaur "eggs" and simulated forests with twigs and branches; when the "babies" hatched (into small plastic dinosaurs) the boys provided "food," cleaned their habitats, and cared for them as if they were dolls. Already aware that "boys don't play with dolls," this context gave them the chance to enact tender family roles and express their affectionate and nurturing emotions.

Wilbur reflected on dinosaurs in the classroom:

◄ These extinct beasts are now reduced to plastic toys. What better allies? Ergo, Louis settles Junior Tyrannosaurus into the classroom dinosaur pit, a large cardboard carton in which he has placed rocks, dirt, branches, and a bed for Junior and his siblings.

Dinosaurs are particularly appealing to young children for very good reasons. The powerful, the monstrous, so they are told, died out long ago. Thus one can gain ascendancy over them. The children can imagine their fearsome being, yet they know that their play with dinosaurs will not have consequences in their own lives.

On the other hand, death is incomprehensible, literally, and unacceptable to children. Could the monsters get resurrected? That pleasant quiver of fear can be safely indulged while being involved in the astounding events of the world. ➤

The creatures from long ago captured the children's interest and curiosity, and many were able to memorize and identify the names of various species. They researched the dinosaurs' habits and habitats, made drawings, and told stories about them. In Wilbur's record of a conversation on the topic of evolution, we see minds at play, grappling with questions and ideas about how the world works.

A teacher is talking with Jimmy (seven years old) about a picture they have seen in a science book. In the course of the discussion, the teacher mentions that metal is found in the earth. Lorin (also seven) joined in the discussion.

Jimmy: I thought machines made metal.

Lorin: What do they make machines from which make the metal?

Jimmy: Wood and things in the olden days. How could stones turn to metal? Monkeys don't turn into men.

Lorin: As a matter of fact, monkeys did turn into men.

Jimmy: How could that be? That's impossible.

Lorin: Millions and millions of years ago, monkeys changed and then their children changed.

Jimmy: How could a tail that grows outside grow inside?

Lorin: It happened over many years. First monkey's children's tails got smaller, and then their children's tails got smaller.

Jimmy: How could one monkey turn into a man?

Lorin: I'm not talking about one monkey. I'm talking about millions of monkeys…

Though Jimmy and Lorin have varying levels of information about the facts at this point, their interest and curiosity propel them to have a dialogue and raise questions.

Dinosaur page.

Science: Children's Discoveries

Over time, with thinking, discussing, absorbing, and interpreting information about the world's phenomena, children form fluid concepts about the nature of reality and their own place in time and the evolving world. By linking the children's natural learning process to school experiences and activities, we hoped they would gain the mastery and confidence they needed to cope with the demands of the rapidly changing twentieth century and beyond.

Serendipity: A Story from Wilbur's Files

I conclude this chapter with a story Wilbur recounted. It begins with a diffident child's interest in guinea pigs and develops into an integrated learning experience involving science, social studies, construction, and social skills.

Wilbur wrote:

◄ Classrooms are thought to be environments of learning. Alas, between the dream and the reality, to paraphrase George Eliot, falls the shadow of children's experience. All too often, schools are rigid places transmitting piecemeal knowledge through rote methods. Such settings stifle what is primary: the child's interest and exuberance and his inherent desire to learn.

In contrast, an interactive environment suited to children's learning styles carries with it the potential of serendipity: of bringing the disaffected child back to himself, to the openness and vitality of childhood. I say "serendipitous" in that the conjunction of specific events attracting the child cannot be prescribed in advance. What is required is a rich mix of available opportunities, a variety of activities from which the child unselfconsciously elicits that most suitable for self-remediation. David's story, below, is a case in point.

David (six years old) joined our group in the middle of the term, having spent a few calamitous months in another private school. When he began attending our school, he spent his time actively looking about, noticing how other children and adults disported themselves, but staying clear of any direct involvement in activities.

David was drawn to the woodworking area where he stood by, observing his classmates absorbed in sawing, drilling, and gluing wood to make constructions. Though the tools were available throughout the day, David did not use them and maintained a surly, suspicious attitude.

One morning, as he leaned against the workbench, quietly watching another child sawing, I asked, "Do you like woodworking?"

David thought about this for a moment, then answered with typical six-year-old obliqueness. "In the other school, you always had to make a clock or something."

Suddenly, I saw myself in Junior High School making the mandated lamp. I thought it quite ugly, but I was determined to complete the project. While boring a hole for the wire to go through the center of the lamp's stem, I managed to drill through the side. Disgrace. Ruination. The instructor responded with copious remarks about how I had not used the tools properly. In that class, I learned very little about how to use tools and a great deal about frustration and embarrassment.

I returned to the present and put aside my ruminations. Being interested in how children conceive of their own behaviors, I asked David: "Do you think it's unusual not to want to make what the teacher selects?" He considered this as carefully as he had my previous question and replied, "It might be unusual for some kids, but it's not unusual for me."

I am happy to report that shortly after this, two events merged, precipitating David into woodworking. He apparently came to believe he would be allowed to make whatever, within reason, he wished. He also came to be immensely fond of our then resident guinea pigs, Peter and Florence.

Gradually, through a chain of disparate events and the benefit of human care and ingenuity, David, guinea pigs, and woodworking meshed into a happy conjunction. It began when David became curious about the activities of the Fresh Food Committee—a self-chosen threesome that visited a local grocery store to collect discarded outer lettuce leaves for the guinea pigs' dietary sustenance. David asked to accompany the group and then join. He was accepted and from then on worked diligently tending to the needs of Florence and Peter.

One day, when he removed the couple from their hutch to feed them a goody—a carrot he had brought from home—David wondered: "Why do Peter and Florence have to always stay on the third floor while the kids can move around the building? I think they need a house where they can go on "vacation.""

He now conceived of his own project and, confident that he could use the workbench for his purposes, he proceeded to construct a "house." He built a large rectangular box with a partition wall dividing it into two equal parts. After placing some alfalfa on its floor and situating Peter and Flo within, he allowed with some satisfaction that they were extraordinarily pleased with their new quarters. And though it takes a remarkable expert to determine when a guinea pig is pleased, no one was prepared to question David's credentials regarding the matter.

"David, did you know that Americans often move to new places?" I asked as we contemplated the new home. David's imagination was at work as he responded:

"Yeah! Well, the guinea pigs are born in America and they should be able to do the same thing. I'll make this into a mobile home so they can move around."

We removed wheels from a defunct shopping cart we found in the street and, after several experiments, attached them to the house.

David: "Hey! How is the house going to move? The guinea pigs can't pull it! I know, I'll pull it with a rope."

David bored two holes into the front wall and knotted a rope he slipped through them. Now Flo and Peter could be pulled from room to room, and from floor to floor.

By this time, and very little time was needed, a litter of fresh guinea pigs arrived. To celebrate this, and in the interest of parity in space, David built a second floor complete with a ramp leading up from the first floor. As his work proceeded, David realized that by knocking out the partition of the first floor and cutting a door into the outer wall, the guinea pigs would be afforded an easier social arrangement. He hinged the door into place and attached a magnetic latch to make sure it was secure.

When he peered through the open door, David exclaimed: "It's so dark in there! The second floor is blocking all the light." He tried to solve the problem by drilling "portholes" into the sides with a brace and bit, but that didn't help much. He pondered for a while and came up with a new idea.

"I think we need electric lights in there," he told me. With assistance, he rigged a battery, wire, socket, and bulb, operated by an outside switch. It was common knowledge that guinea pigs would chew on anything resilient and David carefully shielded the wires with metallic tape.

"Ah, I can see they like it," said David, as he clicked on the light switch.

"What if they chew on the wires and electrocute themselves?" said Danny.

"Not enough charge – one and a half volts," David said. "They won't even feel it."

David, too, liked the bright, safe "vacation" home he designed for the guinea pigs; in a metaphorical sense, it seemed a home for himself.

Subsequently, several litters were born, and David developed a special affinity with a black guinea pig he named Clarence the Greatest. David liked to carry Clarence around the school and show him block buildings and space stations. According to students of guinea pig behavior, the creatures enjoy being held and talked to by humans.

Science: Children's Discoveries

By observing how the guinea pigs related to each other and reacted to clues in their environment, David discovered a way to communicate with them. One morning, David picked up his favorite, and, stroking Clarence's fur gently till he purred, he asked:

"Look, you wanna hear guinea pig language?"

He rustled a paper bag of sunflower seeds and grain. Clarence and the guinea pigs in their hutch became agitated and made guttural, squeaky sounds known as wheeking.

"This means: we want food!" David translated for the kids who had come to watch. He distributed the grain, and quiet returned to the guinea pigs' domain.

I explained to him, "The guinea pigs make wheeking sounds when they hear sounds that they've heard when food is coming. It's called a conditioned reflex." We discussed Pavlov's experiments and observations, and I pointed out to David that he discovered conditioned reflexes on his own.

"Yeah! It happens every time," he responded. Other children wanted to test this out and repeated the experiment on their own. Of course, we had to be careful not to overfeed the guinea pigs for the sake of science.

Recently, reading the works of the eminent biologist George Wald, I wondered if there might be similarities between the serendipitous course of events in David's story and the way the world changes and evolves.

George Wald wrote that "Organic design works by continuous selection among random variations. The organic process at first sight seems slow and very wasteful, but we should think well of it, for it has given us the most intricate mechanism we know. The most complex computers are child's play compared to the simplest living cell. This is the way that not only anatomy but also behavior develops. An organism cannot tolerate clumsy behavior any more than it can tolerate faulty anatomy."

We suspect these remarks can be applied to David's initial as well as his subsequent behavior. In his first school, the teacher, certainly well-meaning and following a rigidly programmed design, chose projects that would develop skills and discipline by assigning required tasks. This program worked for some children, but David, for his own reasons, could not fulfill these assignments. He felt that adults knew very little about his needs, and he withdrew from the "mini-society" of his former school.

Realigned in a new setting, the slow and "continuous selection among random variations" brought about the very goals we hoped to reach. David not only asserted his initiative and ingenuity, but also expanded his skills by learning how to build with tools, hinge a door, attach a latch, wire a lighting system, and study guinea pig psychology.

David's behavior was no longer "unusual," as he was not working against the situation he was in. He came to accept it and be accepted. He could be himself, and his surliness was replaced with enjoyment in conversing with his classmates, teachers, and guinea pigs. He moved from being an observer to participant and gained a new deepening understanding of the world's phenomena. ►

Though teachers are not therapists, Wilbur's interactions and dialogue with David helped David to trust himself and develop his natural talents and interests, as well as feel part of the school community. David and Wilbur's relationship can be characterized by what Vygotsky called a "cognitive apprenticeship," in which an experienced person engages with another by modeling, coaching, articulating, exploring, and reflecting. Through this process, the novice is able to move his incipient knowledge (zone of proximal development) to a state of realization. In this environment, David's own imagination took hold and created the tools he needed to fulfill his inner needs and dreams.

Robert Dewey, who graduated from the school and is presently a conservation activist, writes, "While lots of experiences help to shape who we are, I like to think the 15th Street School's strong emphasis on promoting independent thinking significantly contributed to my personal qualities. I consider myself very intentional about the decisions I make and the way I live my life. I'm also confident in my decision-making and leadership. I believe I've had these qualities for as long as I can remember. They are perhaps most evident in my decision to devote my career to advocating for policies to better protect our nation's natural resources. Also in my specific job, which involves helping to manage a national non-profit natural resources conservation organization."

Robert.

Science: Children's Discoveries

The teacher is not in the school to impose certain ideas
or to form certain habits in the child,
but is there as a member of the community
to select the influences which shall affect and assist him
in properly responding to these influences.

– John Dewey

Chapter 6
Social Studies

The progressive era of the 1920s was a time of change. Einstein's and Freud's theories had altered the perception of space and time and human nature. Planes left the earth and rose into the air, women discarded their corsets and voted, artists went out of their studios to paint *en plein air*, and progressive schools abandoned screwed down-desks for active, learner-oriented classrooms.

Influenced by John Dewey's philosophy of progressive education, the educators Caroline Pratt and Lucy Sprague Mitchell founded the City and Country School in New York City. Along with their teachers, they forged new methods for teaching and learning. Instead of inculcating prepared information from textbooks, teachers joined with their students to create their own curricula. Stepping out of their classrooms, they explored their environment and visited neighborhood shops, fire and police stations. They rode on buses and subways to the harbor, train stations, and bridges, and spoke with shopkeepers, fire fighters, police officers, and train and boat operators. They connected to the complex fabric of interactions that made their city work.

Back in school, they recorded the information they gathered, discussed it, read, and wrote about it, built with blocks and wood, dramatized, drew and mapped their experiences. They researched topics through books, publications, and interviews. They were "learning by doing," and expanding their thinking, reading, writing, and math skills.

These activities, referred to as Social Studies, centered primarily around events involving human interaction and the environments in which they took place. To this day, Social Studies occupies a central place in the progressive education curriculum. Topics are developed around current experiences, such as visiting a friendly store in the area, observing a new building taking shape, or broader themes, such as The Harbor, How We Get Our Food, or Community Workers. These research methods are adaptable to rural and other settings as well as to the study of life in other periods and cultures, such as The Lenape, the original inhabitants of Manhattan.

When I first worked with Wilbur at the Boardman School, he used the theme of transportation for an in-depth class study.

Social Studies at the Fifteenth Street School

Wilbur wrote about Social Studies:
◄ Social studies encompass the study of history, geography, anthropology, economics, law and a variety of inquiry about the groupings and interactions between humans. These interactions are expressed in the day-to-day life of the individuals whose labor supports the goods and services that sustain the urban and rural economies in which they live.

For children, in the early years, the most frequent topic selections for social studies are bits and pieces relating to the children's immediate environment: investigating community helpers with visits to the police and fire stations, the local grocery store, observing the neighborhood on walks, with group trips to the docks, the bridges, the airports, the tunnels, the railroad station. ►

At the Fifteenth Street School, social studies played an important role and took on its own character. We did not follow the progressive school format of developing a central theme with the group and requiring children to be assigned specific tasks and research topics. At our school, the teachers and students were involved in overlapping studies, such as trips to the harbor and follow-up activities, studies of history and other cultures, as well as the children's own Farm of the Six, Troll City, or other projects. We did not impose time limits on the children's engagement with themes they chose or that the teachers introduced.

Watching tugboat activity from
the Staten Island ferry.

Social Studies

Trips we have taken.

Learning About Our City

Wilbur's thoughts:

◄ Living in New York City, we had access to Manhattan's rich, engaging resources for exploration and learning. On our trips on the Staten Island Ferry, we could see Manhattan and learn that it is an island bounded by the East River on the east, the mighty Hudson on the west, and the Harlem River on the north. We visited the harbor at Manhattan's southern end, where the East River and the Hudson meet to form the bay that opens to the Atlantic Ocean. The Hudson is an estuary directly from the sea, moving salt water as far north as Albany, allowing passage to sea bass, eels, and other water travelers.

At the harbor we were treated to a variety of sights and sounds: the Fulton Fish Market and the marvel of ships traveling the waterways. We saw fishing boats, ocean liners, and Navy ships parading on patriotic holidays. We watched the valiant sturdy tugboats pulling large ships in and out of their berths along the river, the scows carrying trash to be deposited in the ocean, oil tankers silently making their way to and fro, cargo ships with buoys and hoists; and the dock workers on shore. On one of our visits, we were favored with an invitation by a tugboat captain to visit his ship. He showed us around and told stories of life aboard his boat.

We saw the lighthouse portrayed in various children's storybooks, resting calmly below the George Washington Bridge, and smelled the odor of briny waters. Leading to and from the city we saw bridges, tunnels, roads, subways, and trains while sleek passenger planes and humpback helicopters landed and departed from airports. There is movement everywhere; the island is a cauldron of bustling machines and the hurried people who service them; in short, all that the children will become familiar with in the process of growing up.

The content of children's work, assuming they are allowed to follow it freely—with a light touch of the adult as collaborator—will embrace the world about themselves—the "here and now" of family, neighborhood, city, farm, town. But the

Social Studies

caveat is that the "here and now" will extend beyond the classroom to the major and significant events in the larger world, the time/space of long ago, as in the prehistoric beasts in the Museum of Natural History, distant habitats and their inhabitants, the past and present life of Native Americans and other cultures, and the here-and-now of space, the immediacy of the constant enterprise of nations at war. Vietnam: the pros and cons of it.

All of these events can be dealt with and comprehended with the appropriate metaphor, re-created in expression that can be *in*scaped rather than *es*caped. ➤

We explored the neighborhood, took trips to parks and around the city, and made maps of some locations. These experiences formed a base for research into the workings of the city and its social fabric. The teachers and children discussed and reflected upon their experiences and the children interpreted their impressions through drawings, stories, dramas, and constructions.

Learning About History

On one of our outings, we visited the liner *Queen Elizabeth* berthed in the harbor and observed the ships and barges navigating the Hudson River. We read about them and about old ships, and Henry Hudson on his ship, the *Half Moon*, discovering the river and sailing up to Albany. Of course, Hudson did not discover the river; Native Americans already inhabited its shore. We read and discussed their history and the story of Manhattan.

The children wanted to know how the world was then, what the events and personalities of their world were at another time. We looked at historical timelines and compared them to their own family timelines to get a perspective. We visited the Museum of Natural History and studied the Native American and Inuit exhibits; read and discussed selections from the *American Heritage Series*, the *How and Why*

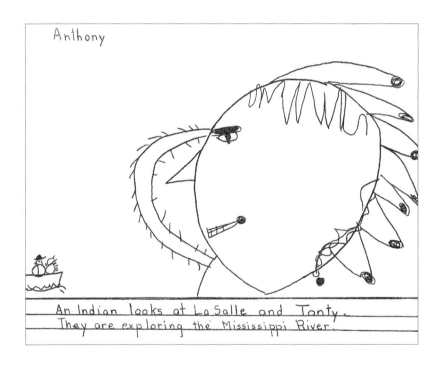

An Indian looks at LaSalle and Tonty.
They are exploring the Mississippi River.

pgs 255-257: Illustrations of American history.

Social Studies

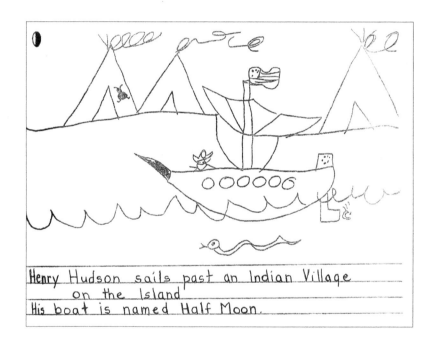

Henry Hudson sails past an Indian Village
on the Island
His boat is named Half Moon.

Paintings of American presidents.

Wonder Books, some *Classics Comics*, and *The First Book of American History*, and looked at maps and globes for reference to locations.

From our readings, some children developed an interest in the Revolutionary War. The idea of freedom from a tyrant was appealing, and some were excited when they found out that the British had been expelled from areas close to where they themselves lived.

We had not banned bringing toy guns to school, and some of the boys enacted scenarios in which they were American soldiers fighting the battles of Staten Island, Brooklyn, and Yorktown Heights. At other times, they were soldiers in WWII. In the Wood Room, they created tents from blocks, boards, and blankets— "camouflaged" hideouts from which they plotted their tactics. They made insignia for their clothes to denote uniforms and marched around the gym. Allan, with his interest in the Civil War, plotted chess-like campaigns with his toy soldiers.

Their understanding of these events derived from books, comics, and talks with adults. At the same time, they could watch the Vietnam War on their TVs, and hearing the comments of parents and friends was part of their everyday lives. The happenings of the present and the past stimulated their imaginations. In school, we discussed these conflicts and their related issues. Interestingly, the children did not enact the Vietnam War in their play.

Children, mostly boys, have always engaged in "war play" outside of school. Bringing it into the school was a radical departure from common practice, and we were concerned how it would develop. Yet, we felt that the children should be allowed to interpret the historical and current events in their own way. We would be able to monitor, discuss, and make suggestions about their activities as they occurred.

Bill Schenker, who attended the school, wrote that "We called our war play Army. I only remember reenacting WWII. I can't remember who specifically played the Allies and who played the Germans, but both sides were represented well: plenty of kids were willing to play the Germans. There was never a feeling of their being inferior or the losers; on the contrary, the Germans were considered to be formidable soldiers and therefore no shame in 'being' one.

Social Studies

"I am clear that I, and perhaps most if not all of us, had no awareness of the Nazi atrocities. It was clear, however, that when you played an American, you were the 'good guys' and when you played a German you were the 'bad guys,' but there was no stigma attached to playing a bad guy. And honestly, I don't remember which side would 'win.' It may have very well been equally both the Allies and the Axis powers! It seemed, certainly for me, that it was more the 'challenge of the game' and 'surviving,' rather than winning that was important.

"BTW: despite my terrific interest in all things Army during that time, I grew up to be a war hating bleeding heart Liberal."

Playing soldiers in a war is another role children assume when they engage in their spontaneous "dramatic play." It's similar to playing house or enacting roles of family members, nurses, doctors, astronauts, and animals, using their imaginations to transform current and past events into spontaneous scenarios. The children know the realities of war, and in their play they can imagine the emotions that characterize the events. As in their stories, they could experience these danger-laden imaginings: allegories for the struggle of living, free of real-life consequences. We monitored this play, being interested in where the kids would go with it. They always remained in the contained "safety zone" of make-believe. Despite the initial interest, these activities did not draw in many kids.

As always, we provided comments, discussions, props, and books. For our library, we obtained a recording of Civil War-era songs, and Wilbur (a native of Tennessee) recounted tales of his early life and of his family at various periods in the history of the South. Certainly, issues of conflict, including slavery, entered into the discussions. I don't recall how much he shared about his experiences in the navy and his subsequent activities in the War Resisters' League. In the European sector, I shared some stories of my growing up in Belgium and coming to America during WWII.

Wilbur recorded an exchange about the children's war play:

◄ Sometimes, visitors are upset that the children are allowed to play the kinds of things children given free choice have always played, especially that they are playing "war" in the gym. They become critical of our unwillingness to suppress or redirect this play.

Voices of Children

Allan plans a campaign with toy soldiers.

Social Studies

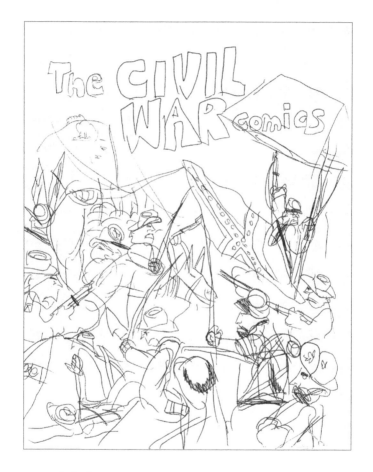

left & right: Allan's cartoon commentaries
on war.

Voices of Children

Social Studies

"Don't they," one of the visitors asks, "have any idea that war is awful?" "Ask them," I suggest.

Allan was shockingly frank. "You think I'm crazy? You could get killed!" His manner suggests that he thinks perhaps his interrogator who asked him whether he would like to be a soldier fighting in a war is, in fact, crazy himself. He takes off his helmet, wipes the perspiration off his brow, and returns to the game. "War is awful," he says. Later, he turned to me in puzzlement.

"Didn't he realize we were playing?" ➤

Allan drew many illustrations and cartoons with Civil War themes, as well as contemporary events, with an uncanny awareness of the irony in human behavior. Others also drew war cartoons, and one depicts warships blasting Beatles songs over loudspeakers to a North Vietnamese warship, hoping to win them over with the power of music.

The places where children perceive teamwork in action is in the military, the NASA teams, sports, the activity of firemen, mostly male-oriented activities. Interestingly, girls did not participate in this play as nurses or members of the military such as WACS and WAVES. Had we been more aware, we might have brought in the stories of Florence Nightingale, Clara Barton and the role of women in WWII and Vietnam. Undoubtedly, soldiers, astronauts, and politicians are perceived as the most powerful members of our society. How their power plays out and the issues and moral concerns underlying events are subject to discussion and reflection. Through their readings, TV reports, and their own enactments of roles, children can gain some idea of the influence and of the responsibilities these figures bear, along with insights into the events and people that shape their world and its values.

The children were interested in what was currently taking place and liked to muse about vanished times, the "olden days" before the advent of TV, all the way to the time of dinosaurs, or the creation of the universe, and forward to their own futures, with space exploration representing the furthest reaches into time and space.

Social Studies and School Life

While we learn about the social world, who the players are, and what governs them, we also include the social world within the school: how the participants perceive each other and function together.

Wilbur wrote about this concept:

◄ One may wonder as to what we "teach" in the school, where, according to our critics, "the children are allowed to do anything they want." The core is Social Studies. It involves our relationship to the outside world as well as the institutions and groups in which we participate (in this instance, the Fifteenth Street School).

Thus, social studies becomes the study of power and its benefits: who is eligible and who is left out within the structure of social groups, and how does it affect individuals and the group. The Fifteenth Street School Program was an attempt to bring awareness of each person's identity and actions into his/her actual social situation. The level of discourse on the part of the children, most of it self-regulative, was an expression of their own decision-making process—such as choosing who would be in the play presented in the gym, and how to proceed. Many times, we were surprised and delighted by how the children were able to take initiative to create a play, practice in it, and declare that they were ready to present it without conferring with an adult. ►

Children have always congregated in their own fluid groups outside of school and before schools even existed. They invent and direct their own games, plays, songs, and projects. On the negative side, such groups can develop into gangs.

No one knows the exact dynamic of such associations – how are similar ideas formed, transformed, and transmitted from one mind to another? How is consensus reached? How are plans articulated, organized, implemented, and communicated to parties outside the group? At the Fifteenth Street School, we sought to create the circumstances to enhance the possibilities for the formation of self-determining structures by the children. We hoped that the concepts stemming from these experiences would expand the children's capacities for autonomous action and social awareness. Not all the students were involved in all activities, but generally everyone knew about them through word of mouth and announcements, fliers, and posters or *The Squeaker Times.*

Social Studies Themes

Following are examples of social studies themes relating to how the children and teachers developed constructs to deal with their social concerns within and outside the school.

Given the political climate and elections of the time, the children decided to recreate the larger world within the dimensions of their domain and conduct their own imaginary elections. The guinea pigs once again became surrogates for worldly figures. From the present litter, the children selected two and named them Johnson and Kennedy to run in a presidential election (Johnson was actually president in 1966, and, though Kennedy had been assassinated in 1963, they resurrected his memory to run one more time). The children initiated a campaign and prepared fliers for each candidate.

Wilbur described the campaign:

◄ Three children are the main promoters of this school event. They have set up the tape recorder and gone through the building to announce that there will be speeches by Johnson and Kennedy. A small crowd has gathered to hear and respond to the children who speak for the candidates.

Announcer: This broadcast has been brought to you by WABC, WPIX, WNEN, WOR. It will be on for two hours during the election of Johnson and Kennedy for president.

Johnson: This is Johnson. I am going to make things better, sports, golf, more exciting. I'll make submarines better, lights better, flags better, loud speakers better.

(Cries of yeas and boos from the audience.)

Thank you. I'll make cars better, subways better, landing on the moon shot better by 1968 or maybe by 1969. I'll try. I can't promise you.

Voices of Children

(Clapping of hands, boos, shouts of approval.)

Kennedy: I am Kennedy. I hope you will make me president. I'll make our navy more powerful, more stronger against Vietnam.

(Boos and yeas.)

Kennedy: So we can fight Vietnam, I'll make our marines more stronger, more carriers to make our country more stronger against any bad people. Also to help you save water. We must save water. When you wash dishes or take a bath, don't leave the water running.

(Cries of approval.)

Kennedy: So vote for me, Kennedy. I shall give more police to protect you from night robbers and all the bad people, so vote for me.

(Shouts of approval intermingled with boos.)

Announcer: This has been live coverage. The end.

Thus, history is contemporaneity, and one participates in it.

Finally, Election Day arrived and the students cast paper ballots into a cardboard box. When Kennedy won, he was gleefully paraded through the school. "I'll make our country stronger, have more police to protect you, and save water."

▶

From the debates they have seen on TV, the children grasp the concept of organizing a political campaign and establishing a forum for stating problems and propose their solutions. They know that those who seek to rule must articulate important issues. They must take stands and convince those they represent of the validity of their points of view. The children understand some of the essential elements of political life. The candidates' promises reflect concerns of actual current events, and they are responsible for their resolution.

"I'll make cars better, subways better, landing on the moon shot better by 1968, or maybe by 1969. I'll try. I can't promise you."

They must deal with national security: " So we can fight Vietnam, I'll make our Marines more stronger, more carriers to make our country more stronger against any bad people."

Social Studies

(Interesting, as most school families were opposed to the war. They may be mimicking politicians with these opinions.)

They must set rational policies and enlist the public to follow them: "Also to help you save water. We must save water. When you wash dishes or take a bath, don't leave the water running."

The children created their own imaginative analogy for the workings of the world. They imagined what it's like to take responsibility for governance.

Troll City

In the mid 1960's, Troll figures became popular. They came in many sizes and costumes, had the same impish shape, and no gender. Most of the kids owned at least one; they liked to comb and caress their brightly colored hair, somewhat like petting an animal. When the trolls came to school, they became actors in the children's imaginary games.

Allison brought a cardboard box and asked Wilbur to help her shape it into an apartment for her troll. "How about we cut the box in half?" he said. "And if you take off one side it will be easier to work in it." Allison painted it and made furnishings from wood scraps and found objects. Other trolls also needed homes. "Can I make one too?" their owners asked. We took a trip to the neighborhood liquor store, where they gave us empty boxes. The kids decorated and painted them to make homes for their trolls and their families. They stacked the boxes on top of each other on a table in the Wood Room to form an apartment building. Soon there were so many, the kids started another stack and formed two buildings. As the structures grew, someone called the complex Troll City.

On her map of Troll City (p272), Celia listed various municipal services and agencies: an art gallery, a museum, greenhouses, an aquarium, a zoo, a school, and apartment buildings, and surprisingly – no shops. I don't recall whether there was an actual zoo or school in Troll City or whether they existed only on the map.

Into this environment, the children brought their knowledge and observations of the real world and transformed the trolls into citizens, politicians, hippies, and entertainers. They reported the troll's doings in a miniature-sized newspaper called *The New York Troll*. At some point, they decided that Troll City, with its many inhabitants and homes, needed a mayor.

Wilbur wrote about the election and how some Troll City problems were managed:

◄ I begin with Troll City and a flurry of activity, as the children have decided to set up an imaginary campaign for electing a Troll mayor. Two trolls are selected to run, and they deliver their speeches through child surrogates:

"Vote for me. I'll be your best friend!"

"If you help me win, I'll invite you to my birthday party." This was politicking on the child's level, born of speeches, of course, heard at home on the television set during coverage of local and national elections.

In a story for The New York Troll David noted that the Mayor had only three days to fulfill promises he made in his campaign. When he failed to do so, someone complained,

"It's not fair, the Mayor proposed an elevator for Troll City, and he hasn't done a thing yet!"

"Yeah, and what about the swimming pool?"

Anthony suggests, "Demand impeachment!"

More discussions.

"Should he have a second chance?"

We, the teachers, raise the question of how such problems are handled in the real world. To follow up, I spoke to Judge Schwartz, of the New York City civil court and arranged to take a trip to his office on the edge of Wall Street. As we are ushered into his study, the children confront him with questions: What does he do when…? What happens when people don't agree? Who wins? Who loses?

He is a rarity: a good listener. We are interested. An actual trial (it had been planned that way) at which he is the judge is called. He slips on a robe. We enter the courtroom. It's about a car collision. Two versions are given. How and

Social Studies

what to decide? Judge Schwartz addresses both parties with equanimity and respect. And after much talk, he announces an amicable settlement. The children are impressed. Back to his chambers. Then comes the denouement:

Judge Schwartz: "The million-dollar question for judges is how to combine these things: patience and what we call principles; that is, justice and mercy. Justice means to do the right thing for all parties. Sometimes it begins with thoughts of punishment, but above all we seek mercy. We try not to holler, put down either party. You know what dignity is? You know how you feel blue, low, when you're treated unfairly? We try to avoid that. Mercy is most of all treating those who committed a crime with dignity. The best of judges show respect in their attitude—the way they act toward the victim and the guilty in the hope that both will eventually come to a better and clear understanding. So my advice to you is this: patiently talk it over with your mayor and see if you can't reach an agreement that everyone is satisfied with. It's not always easy, but you can try."

Judge Schwartz' words made an impression.

"Never knew what mercy was before," Eric says. "Now, I know."

"What is it?" Sarah asks.

"It's, you know, like being fair."

The first step toward understanding a complicated, complex human affair.

Back to school. Soon, with help, Danny builds an elevator: a small box with strings attached to a pulley moving up and down and stopping at various floors. A swimming pool is provided. The children are pleased, knowing that the trolls are happy and that all is quiet and peaceful in luxurious Troll City. ►

Interacting with Judge Schwartz, the children gained insights into the workings of the law and the responsibilities of citizenship.

Troll City in a bookshelf.

Social Studies

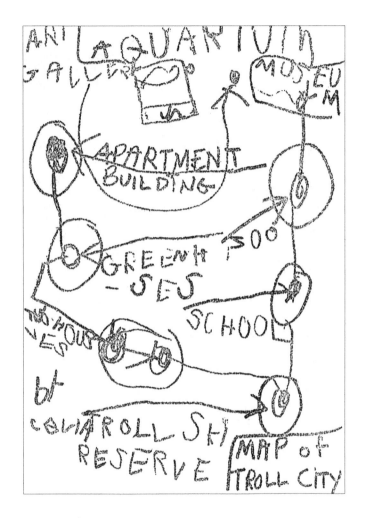

left & right: Troll City map and newspaper:
The New York Troll.

THE NEW YORK TROLL

TROLL Mayor

Danny's Troll ran for Mayor and won.

He has 3 more days to complete a few more things that he promised in his election.

by David Schwartz

NEWS

① A house will be moved from Troll City to Fur City today.

Jennifer

② I announce the birth of a new bean in 2nd grade Troll City's greenhouse

by Celia

Social Studies

The Squeaker Times

TROLL INTERVIEWS
by Lynn and Rachel

Trollie with blue hair. Trollie lives in new york. He works on his rocket ships. It snowed on his trip to trollsville.

Jennifer S. David Z anes, Michele, Laura, Kathy and David were painting the troll houses.

Painting the troll houses.

This is Chris' Trollie and his rocket

More Troll news.

Voices of Children

"It's, you know, like being fair." Again, the children had cooperated and expanded their skills to develop a complex structure woven out of the real world and imagination. Through their scenarios, they interpreted important events, relived the past, and projected the future.

Troll City continued to grow, and when the stacks of boxes were in danger of toppling, the children moved the Trolls and their furnishings onto a shelf we provided. Eventually, Troll City was replaced with other projects, and it became a museum itself.

The Problem-Solving Committee

According to A.S. Neill, "Self-regulation means behavior coming from the self, not from outside compulsion, and extended to the social group becomes self-government."

At our school, the structure we had established for settling disputes worked well. At a meeting, while discussing problems, Wilbur suggested: "Allan, you complain that Terry keeps teasing you, and Terry complains that you won't let him read your comic books. Maybe a few of you could get together and have your own meeting to figure this out."

"Yeah! That's a good idea," they said.

The next day, a small group of girls and boys gathered in the Art Room. Though it was the children's meeting, Wilbur and I sat in to take notes and assist. "We're here for a meeting about settling problems. Wilbur and I are going to take notes," I told them.

Matty: "Yeah. When kids complain, we'll talk with them."

Wilbur: "That sounds good. Remember Judge Schwartz and how the court tried to solve problems?"

For the next hour they talked about problems and everyone had ideas for dealing with them. Without articulating the concept, some children came up with general rules not only for solving problems, but also for preventing their occurrence.

Marina said, "Hey! This is about solving problems. Let's call it the Problem-Solving Committee." They had become a group with a purpose. Wilbur and I worked with them to schematize their thoughts into a document. They also elected five committee members and six advisors to the committee. Their functions would be determined at another time.

Wilbur reflected on the children's ideas:

◄ The children articulated the rules for the committee in two manifestos. The first set of rules is mostly 'don'ts.' The following set is stated in positive terms. Why so generous? Why so non-punitive? The teachers assumed irrational social behavior derives from a feeling of loneliness, separation or need. Given this, the remedy was attending to the feeling and not furthering the sense of unhappiness or separateness by punitive means. By the time the "rule makers" are seven, the children have been in school two years and have incorporated its values and ethos. The process was not one of inculcation but bringing to the fore what already existed. ►

In all our years of teaching, we had never seen this kind of development in self-governance. Wilbur and I looked at each other.

"Can you believe how amazing this is?"

We felt we were witnessing the Founding Children develop their own constitution. I copied the rules on mimeograph stencils and printed them for the whole class. At a group meeting, we discussed the rules and the functions of the committee. Everyone agreed with the committee's policies, and without much ado, it went into action. At first it was very casual, as anyone could call on any committee member at any time. The committee held meetings to discuss how to proceed with their tasks.

"When there's a problem, they can call three of us together."

"Yeah. And try to find a quiet place to talk."

This did, in fact, work out. As the "three" heard the complaint, most of the time, they were able to articulate the problem, suggest alternatives and attain a successful resolution. Sometimes a teacher participated to listen or offer suggestions. Many kids wanted to try their hand at problem solving and joined the committee as rotating members. At times, their meetings took a humorous turn, as kids giggled or suggested outrageous solutions.

Rules of the Committee

1. Don't be funny (this means that the committee should be taken seriously and is an authoritative body).
2. Don't hit.
2. Don't be wild and silly.
4. Don't tease.
5. Don't pick fights just to call the committee. You should be nice and try to calm them down in a nice way, so they won't do it again.

other things the committee can do:

1. Help people make things.
2. Water the plants every day and water other people's plants, too.
3. Help people read in the morning.
4. Erase the board.
5. Give people information—like where the paper is.
6. Clean up stuff.
7. Fix people up when they get hurt.
8. Cheer them up when they get hurt – like tell them funny things.
9. Help animals – like with broken legs.
10. When people get hurt make a place for them on the couch and help them lie down, put a pillow under their head and put a cover on them.

Social Studies

Wilbur recorded his conversation with committee members working on a case:

◄ While swinging on the parallel bars, Mary hit Joe with her feet, and he pushed her off the bars, hurting her feelings more than her body.

Committee Member Jerri: Mary says she hit Joe by accident, and I believe her. She doesn't lie. She didn't see him. Joe got mad and pushed her.

Committee Member Maria: So then the committee asked Joe and Mary to go to the room where we could talk in private.

Teacher: Was Joe willing to go?

Committee Member Kathy: He went like this. Ohhh. Ohhh. Ohhh.

Teacher: He didn't want to go, but he did it anyway.

Maria: Yeah. We went upstairs and asked them what happened. We were sitting around the table, all crowded up and suddenly Joe said, "Here's another problem," so, I said, "Table, why aren't you getting bigger?" And then we all started laughing and Jerri said, "Hey, we fixed the problem."

Teacher: Sometimes what you want is get everyone feeling good about being in school again and if you can do this, it can be a solution to the problem.

Kathy: I know we solved the problem, because we were laughing and then Joe said to Mary, "Let's go to the gym and play" and they did.

Teacher: That's a real test. First Joe and Mary are mad at each other, and then they want to play together again. ►

In this episode, the children accepted the concept of settling disputes by following the steps of an arbitration process. The process of finding a solution sparked Maria's imagination to go beyond the established pattern and create another reality. "Table, why aren't you getting bigger?" A parallel view of the problem in an unexpected absurd context makes the original problem lose its power and vanish. Laughter dispels ill will, and normal life resumes. If only such good will and sense could prevail in the world!

Wilbur recorded two more committee cases:

◄ The problem discussed in the following record was about

Terry (newly arrived seven-year-old from another school), who had managed to take most of the gym equipment for his own exclusive use. After discussing how the committee had arranged a more equitable distribution, I questioned the children about their reactions.

Wilbur: When Nick complained that Terry was unfair, did you run to the gym and bully Terry into sharing, because you thought he was greedy? (Wilbur's use of "topsy turvy" humor, here implying that the opposite occurred and no bullying, in fact, took place.)

Bob: No, we listened to both of them and then we said it wasn't fair, and Terry agreed to let Nick have some of the things.

Wilbur: Do you think Nick was happy with the solution?

Sara: He didn't seem to mind.

Wilbur: How about Terry?

Bob: He was happy.

Danny: Half and half.

Wilbur: What do you mean by half and half?

Danny: I can tell, because I'm always playing with him. He didn't like it that much.

Wilbur: Did he agree because he was forced to by the Committee?

Danny: But if he wanted anything, he knew he should take what he got.

Lisa: Something is better than nothing.

Wilbur: I think I know what you mean. Terry still wanted all the toys, but he didn't want to argue with the kids on the committee. ➤

This piece ends abruptly, as it would have been important to hear from Terry. The discussion continues with the description of another problem that the committee was called upon to solve.

◄ In this situation a teacher enters a complaint:

Teacher: If you remember, I entered a complaint. I had left the workroom, and when I came back there were toys on the floor and all over the tables. Things had been left everywhere.

Social Studies

Committee Member Tim: The committee asked the kids in the room if they had left things around, and they said no, but John began to pick some things up.

Teacher: Yes, instead of getting angry and blowing my top like a volcano, I called the committee to try to work on the problem. Then Tim said, "Oh! Let's pick the stuff up," and all of you helped.

Tim: Wasn't that nice of me?

Teacher: It was nice, but the important thing was finding a solution that worked, and the room was cleared. One of the things that has also worked with this committee is that you haven't bullied kids, nor have you interfered with anyone's rights.

Committee Member Michael: Only Sid said he was going to make war on the committee.

Teacher: What about that, Sid?

Sid: The real problem is…. I don't think Tim is going to like to hear this, but he's been bugging me for a long time, and since he's been doing it, I thought I'd pay him back.

Teacher: Were you able to do it?

Sid: Well. No.

Teacher: Perhaps you could have come to the committee and said: "One of your members is teasing me." It is true that sometimes you do tease him, and maybe they could have helped find a solution. The trouble with war is that there are two sides. If you start a war against someone, soon they are fighting you. People just won't let someone else war on them without doing something. Do you feel better about the committee now?

Sid: Yeah.

Teacher: Want to be on the next committee?

Sid: Maybe.

Teacher: Maybe you could ease into it by being a reporter for the next committee meeting. Would you like that?

Sid: O.K.

Teacher: All right, thanks very much for the interview. We now return you to Station Z.A.P.

Voices of Children

One of the premises of the Fifteenth Street School was that self-discipline would be most effective if the children had experienced autonomy in their earliest years. We watched to see what modes and forms the children would develop for regulating school affairs. If teachers did not try to prematurely formalize the children's ideas into rules, they possibly would evolve to genuine, appropriate self-governing forms. In their first experience with rule making, pertaining to the Farm of the Six, the children had articulated the values they held and hoped would prevail in their future world.

The Problem-Solving Committee was an outcome of many informal and group discussions between teachers and students about the behaviors of children and adults, in and out of school, and their rules were a rational expression of that process. ➤

In their authentic voices, the children echoed the wisdom of thinkers and philosophers who seek to make the world a better place. "When people get hurt, make a place for them on the couch and help them lie down, put a pillow under their head and put a cover on them." This time their scenario did have consequences in their world.

The Problem-Solving Committee was the most realized expression of the children's conceptual development in the social/imaginative realm. In these kinds of deliberations, children are involved in a genuine team effort to find equitable solutions, and there are no pat answers. Their minds are struggling with conflict, compromising, and trying to balance personal need and the interest of others. Their acceptance of an orderly exchange, where one listens and reciprocally is heard, where compromise and/or consensus are achieved, demonstrates both the children's grasp of and acquiescence to a form of a social contract between themselves and the requirements for living in a social environment. With their imaginations, judgment, social skills, and sense of responsibility, they instituted a working structure for regulating their own behavior and relationships in their school. They undertook the task with serious intent and optimism, acting as legislators, judges, counselors, and responsible citizens of the society they had participated in creating.

Social Studies

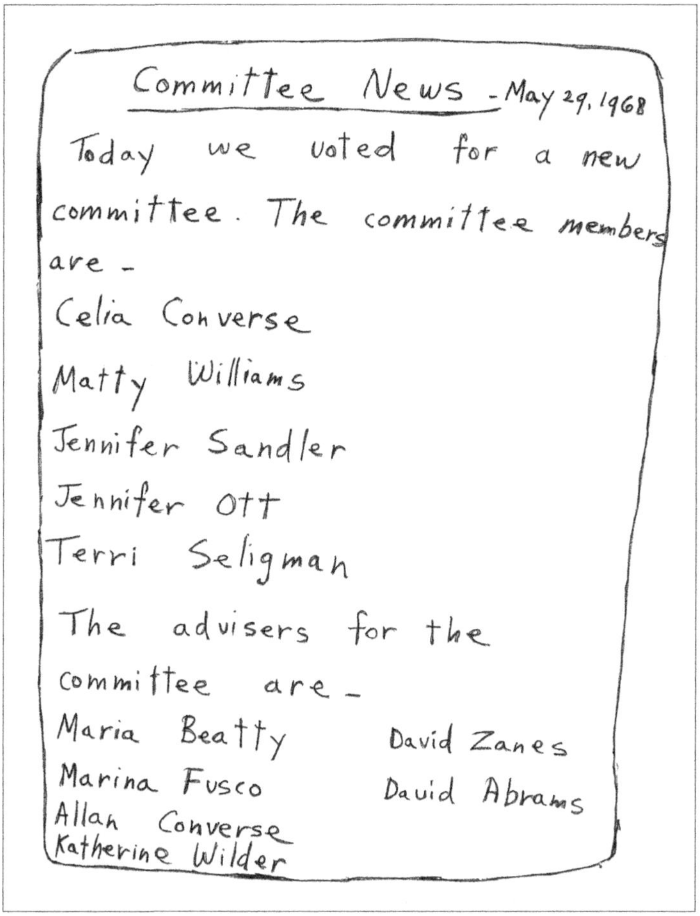

Committee News - May 29, 1968

Today we voted for a new committee. The committee members are -

Celia Converse

Matty Williams

Jennifer Sandler

Jennifer Ott

Terri Seligman

The advisers for the committee are -

Maria Beatty   David Zanes

Marina Fusco   David Abrams

Allan Converse

Katherine Wilder

Committee news.

Voices of Children

Rules of the Committee

1. Don't be funny
2. Don't hit
3. Don't be wild and silly.
4. Don't tease
5. Don't fight with fellow committee members.
6. Don't pick fights just to call the committee.

_____

7. You should be very nice and try to calm them down in a nice way, so they won't do it again

Other things the committee can help with —

1. Help people make things.
2. Water the plants everyday and water other people's plants too.
3. Help people read in the morning.
4. Erase the board.
5. Giving people information - like where the paper is.
6. Cleanup stuff.
7. Fix people up when they get hurt.
8. Cheer them up when they get hurt - like tell them funny things
9.

Rules of the committee.

Minds at Work

In *Mind and Society*, Lev Vygotsky (1978) wrote: "From the point of view of development, creating an imaginary situation can be regarded as creating abstract thought." Through their play with materials and ideas, the children have invoked space exploration, elections, trials, a future ideal farm, and wars. They have considered issues of conflict and means of resolution, as exemplified in the events with the trolls and the judge. In the elections they conducted, they sought to understand representative government and the responsibilities of elected officials and set this knowledge into practice in the Problem-Solving Committee.

Their constructs and studies related to outer space, prehistory, plants and animals, power and mechanics, and the science lab supported the formation of concepts regarding the behavior of earthly and cosmic forces, as well as the behavior and governance of people and their relation to the environment. They engaged in observation and research, raising questions, hypothesizing, testing, and noting results, while also creating metaphoric entities such as guinea pig astronauts and presidents, troll mayors, the future farm, and many stories.

With the Farm of the Six, the Problem-Solving Committee, elections, Troll City, Space Stations, and the library (see chapter 2), the children created cooperative enterprises that served a common purpose. These constructs deal with interests and concerns in the children's immediate world, while reaching to a widening circle of the larger environment in which they live. In considering social and ethical problems, the children seek to apply ideas of law and justice in a non-judgmental, non-punitive manner. These complex, masterful creations reflect the mind at play/at work, living, articulating, and solving problems. Inherent in these activities is the children's search for a moral ground, for understanding how their society functions and how to participate in its growth.

Though not entirely without friction, these self-selected teams of boys and girls functioned with a high level of cooperation, involvement, and positive communication. They created an environment in which ideas are generated in a free-flowing continuum, and choices and decisions are determined by consensual agreement. In some instances, someone having a strong interest or point of view emerged as a leader, yet did not dominate.

All this came about through the children's own motivations and interest, fostered by dialogue with each other, their teachers, families, and friends. When engaged in meaningful activity, the energy of creative endeavor expands their awareness as they move forward with enthusiasm and optimism.

The power of children's imaginations is manifest universally. When given the opportunity, their minds and creative impulses flourish everywhere. I remember in the 1950's Wilbur and I often took walks in lower Manhattan, where many empty lots could be seen. We observed groups of children playing with the debris left there from the houses that had been torn down. The children were absorbed in building low-lying constructions and abstract forms with the bricks, wood, and metal pipes they found. They made stands from which they sold comics and toys. We did worry about nails sticking out, though the children took great care. I no longer have the photos I took of those original, spontaneous assemblies and of the boys and girls who took initiative to build them. I have seen similar activities at beaches and riverfronts, and they probably occur in abandoned sites everywhere.

At a public school where I once taught, the students in a second-grade class, while sitting at screwed-down desks, managed their own "farm" at a table where we brought fruits and vegetables. We researched the topic, and the children wrote and drew about where the produce came from, how it grew and ended up on our plates. I remember marveling at a six-year-old boy who brought drawings he had made on the pages of an old phone book.

Lev Vygotsky has emphasized that learning takes place in a social context. At the Fifteenth Street School, we were amazed at the high level of interaction and collaboration that the children exhibited. Working in self-selected groups, they were developing their abilities to create structures to govern their own life in school. The choices they made in the use of time, space, and the available resources proved they were exercising their capacities at a high level of functioning. It was our hope that these experiences would awaken a sense of wonder and exploration and establish the foundation for further studies.

Social Studies

On the Staten Island ferry.

Social Studies

As well as endorsing his view of the natural development of the child, it could be said that Tolstoy's view also rests on the principle of uncertainty . . .
Traditional forms of education present facts to the student rather than demonstrating that human knowledge grows through revision, collaboration and investigation.

– Dan Moulin

Chapter 7

1964 to 1968 at the Fifteenth Street School

During our first year at the school, we observed the students playing and working as they developed self-reliance and took pride in their achievements as artisans, actors, leaders, caretakers, participants in a community. This is not to say that Utopia had been achieved and everyone felt the same way. Yet, compared with our experience in other schools, we felt a palpable sense of active engagement in the joint enterprise of creating a school where the children belonged and that belonged to them.

Wilbur wrote about the focus of our school:

◄ The work of children consists of the activities they engage in. It can be distinguished from labor or distraction in that it offers satisfaction, pleasure and expansion. It is a way of being in the world actively, while exploring it, and is characterized by discipline, a self-imposed discipline. If the children are playing "Cops and Robbers" and a child is too "bossy," out he/she goes. If one is painting a picture, the edges of the paper provide boundaries that say: "Stop here!" Their play is convention and rule bound.

Vygotsky (1978) wrote, "In one sense a child at play is free to determine his own actions. But in another sense, this is illusory freedom, for his actions are in fact subordinated to the meanings of things, and he acts accordingly."

At our school, the focus is on the educational environment, where children can be engaged in meaningful activity, and finding ways and means of expanding skills: social and intellectual. The children initiated much of what emerged, and sometimes they developed their ideas with little adult assistance. On the other hand, a discussion between children or a child's remark to a teacher might be the start of a new project. We knew some of the interests of children from our previous work, but we had not experienced their depth and breadth that we witnessed at our school. ➤

Perceptions of the School

Visitors to the school expressed a variety of opinions. Some thought of it as a place without any structure, while others decried it as being too structured. One even took exception to an alphabet displayed on the wall.

Wilbur described their reactions:

◄ "And where are the desks? When do the children study?" Some visitors ask as they survey the tables with kids seated at them, some reading, some preparing a stencil, some playing with Cuisenaire rods, while at the easel Margie and Jolie cover the board-size paper with moving color. In a corner of the room, two children have picked a lettuce leaf from a box to entice Peter—daddy guinea pig—to eat, they elicit cuddly sounds of contentment by gently stroking the guineas' fur as well as rasping throaty protests when stroking against the grain.

The response of the conventionalist was not unexpected: "unrealistic" at best and predicting the certainty of chaos, quarreling, and destruction of property. Others thought of it as a romantic notion spawned by followers of Rousseau, a manifestation of mysticism that presumed the virtues of the ever-rational natural savage.

Others were impressed with the atmosphere of high spirits and ease that pervaded the school. The children's involvement, humor, and sense of ownership of their lives were the signs that gave us confidence that we were on the right track. The imposition of adult decrees stands in sharp contrast to the self-regulative functioning of children in situations when playing with each other, without adult intervention or supervision in the groups they form. ➤

Wilbur and I often reflected on the unfolding process of the school's development. We discussed the day-to-day work, as well as the school's overarching philosophy, and welcomed constructive criticism. We were glad to exchange ideas with our colleagues from the Bank Street School for Children, who provided helpful comments. They were amazed at the way the children functioned independently, and subsequently Bank Street advisors assigned student teachers to the school for internships. We discussed our program with the students as well as their advisors when they visited the school. We held meetings with our early childhood staff to deal with specific problems as they occurred, while Orson managed administrative issues regarding admissions and staffing. The children's spirits were high, and so were ours.

Developing the Skills Program

At the end of the first year, we had a sense of a successful launch, though we were concerned with the skills program. We thought that the combination of informal classes and the creative input of the children would provide a breakthrough to learning to read near to grade level. This did not happen. Mastery of skills concerned many parents, and to some extent, the students themselves, as some realized that friends outside were moving ahead of them.

We met with fellow teachers from other schools to discuss these problems and kept abreast of developments in education and new curriculum ideas. We began a review of our Language Arts program and researched current reading programs that could expand and complement it. After much deliberation, we decided to use didactic materials such as sequential workbooks, which, used without pressure, would reinforce the children's abilities to decode words as well as to read fluently.

We selected three available programs to assist with reading strategies and introduced them in the second year. By then, some of the fives had turned six and joined the older group.

The Sullivan Programmed Reader. Sullivan Associates (now operated by Phoenix Learning Resources) designed a program for beginning readers to third graders that focused mainly on decoding. The goal was to keep the child interested in the process of acquiring reading skills, and they designed a series of colorful workbooks with simple story lines and humorous characters in the genre of the famous *Cat in the Hat.* By following instructions, children moved in easy steps to break words into units that were combined to form more complicated words. Children answered questions and could find the correct answers by moving a slider on the page. Gradually, the simple exercises and stories became more complex. In our school, each child owned his or her book and worked independently. Teachers assisted with reviewing and explaining the work when needed.

SRA Science Research Associates Program: This reading series emphasized vocabulary and sentence building as well as comprehension. It consisted of a set of booklets with stories and questions designed to build these skills. Levels of mastery were indicated by colors of the books. As students proceeded through the color sequence, they could read the stories and complete the exercises on their own. Teachers assisted with reviews and suggestions.

Bank Street Reader. Published in 1965, the readers provided easy-to-read stories and vocabulary studies. They were the first readers to deal with urban themes and portray multicultural characters. We also extended our collection of phonics charts, recorded sounds, and word games.

Assessing Didactic Materials

Both the *Sullivan* and *SRA* series were designed to enable students to work independently and move through the material at their own pace. The *Programmed Reader* raised eyebrows among some teachers who visited the school and regarded them as overly structured and close-ended, perhaps seeing them as instruments of Skinnerian behavioral indoctrination. We had our own qualms, but given the school's atmosphere of freedom and creativity we felt that the children would profit from materials they found interesting and challenging and that supported their efforts to read and write. For us, the teachers, they were a respite from constantly having to create original materials. We worked with the children on these programs throughout the day, meeting in small groups or with individuals.

The children took readily to the new materials, especially the *Programmed Reader*. In later years, some of the graduates reported feeling pressured by the *SRA* materials, sometimes skipping ahead to the more advanced colors to keep up with their friends. It didn't matter if they were comfortable with the content. Graduates remember the *Programmed Reader* fondly, and some report still owning their copies.

Graduate Michael Krieg wrote, "I liked the funny, silly characters like Sam and Ann, their dog Nip and cat Tab and it was easy to learn new words, such as pins and pans, jars and jars of jam. Having my own workbook gave me a sense of ownership of the process of learning to read."

Wilbur commented on the reading program:

◄ We found that the Language Arts Program alone was not sufficient to teach the skills. We needed the published workbooks and readers to provide the rules and regularities of language needed for decoding words. To our surprise, we found that the *SRA*, yes, even the bête noire of reading specialists, the *Sullivan Programmed Readers*, offered specific satisfaction. These and the *Bank Street Readers*, handbooks and easy-to-read books, all validate skill building and correspond to the children's image of what is required if they are to learn to read real books effectively.

Completing the self-checking exercises in the *Programmed Readers* and *SRA* allows the children to move ahead at their own pace independently. There is the conquering of this material: it provides the satisfaction of completing a task and tackling the regularities of real books. Finally, it offers an end result: that of mastery certified and of ascertaining one's competencies. Teachers also benefit by being released from

Four Years at the Fifteenth Street School

left & right: Working on the Sullivan Readers:
with a teacher, independently, teaching each other,
and teaching the guinea pigs.

Voices of Children

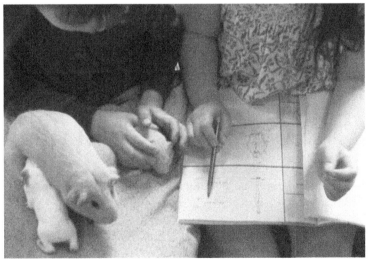

Four Years at the Fifteenth Street School

Michael.

Voices of Children

the task of producing worksheets themselves. They assist the students by monitoring their work, addressing specific omissions or errors such as spelling, and mentoring the alphabet script writing with the transition to cursive. ►

For math, we continued using materials, such as Cuisenaire Rods and Geo-boards and workbooks, as well as engaging in activities such as weighing, graphing, measuring, and estimating.

Learning Levels

We hoped that some of the formal structures we made available would be a bridge connecting language expression and learning to read, for the children and for ourselves.

Wilbur wrote about the issues concerning the skills program:
◄ Though the children's enthusiasm for exploring the world and expressing themselves was still evident, they sensed that the world had other expectations of them. While continuing to engage in their language arts activities, the children were being influenced by tales from their peers and relatives schooled in the conventional modes, by movies and TV shows. These sources conveyed the idea that "real" learning to read and write has to do with an entire class bent on paper or book at their isolated desks.

The students welcomed the new learning materials, which, aside from their intrinsic value, resembled the image of learning they were developing.

Not everyone was equally enthusiastic about learning, and individual inclinations affected each one's level of participation.

The spectrum goes from those who for whatever their own good reasons, and despite ours, engage fully in the activities, and those who are at the opposite pole. Some, at the extremity, seem to pick up the skills by osmosis. They get it immediately and move ahead. At the other end is James, who is seemingly singularly disinterested. There were indications that it was more than a lack of interest.

When he was tested by a specialist at our request, he was deemed dyslexic. His parents immediately agreed to tutorials. He moved slowly, painfully ahead. Between these extreme examples exists the greater number of children who participate and learn at an even pace.

Freedom alone is not so all-healing that it can solve all the concerns that affect a learning environment. Surprised? No. The spectrum exists. ➤

Scheduling Classes for Skills Groups

The students' positive responses to the new materials confirmed that we were on the right track. However, we had trouble keeping up with the instructional groups in reading and math while dealing with all the areas of curriculum and checking what was happening in the gym.

We needed to revise the daily pattern of activities to be more in keeping with the needs and resources of students and teachers. To provide a predictable schedule for everyone, we designated the first morning hour for a reading class and the first afternoon hour for a math class. Wilbur and I each worked with a group based on age and skill level, in each subject. This way, we could gather all the needed materials at once and have free time for other activities without interruption. For the students, attendance was still optional.

In these classes, we followed a format in which various levels could be accommodated during the session. We met with the designated group to introduce or discuss a topic, then with individuals or sub groups, while others worked independently on their workbooks or stories. Each child worked at her/his own level, and we monitored individuals to assess and assist with their needs. As everyone was not, so to speak, on the same page, children did not need to attend regularly to make progress.

Each day, we announced the start of classes. Most students wanted to attend, but some chose to remain in the gym or visit the secretary or the four- to five-year-old group. Some played on the decks and side rooms while the main rooms were used for classes. For the teachers, the regularly scheduled instruction periods were a relief. The children did not perceive the new schedule as a big change; they could still engage in the same activities and free movement as before we instituted classes.

As the second year drew to a close, it seemed that the new structure was providing a sound framework for our group. The reading and math classes in the morning and afternoon were a time for concentrated instruction in those subjects, while work and play continued in other areas throughout the day.

There were, at the time, approximately forty children in the school. A few new students who transferred from other schools usually took time to adapt to the structure. Some flourished, but, much as we tried, the school was not a match for everyone, and some parents withdrew their children from the school.

We continued to strive to refine the environment for learning, seeking out appropriate books and materials to enrich each study area, checking and reviewing how the whole system was functioning. We still hoped that the structure of non-compulsory scheduled classes, free time, and the enriched environment would provide a balanced situation in which the children would learn basic skills, while maintaining their freedom of movement and vitality. We were optimistic about the school's continuing growth.

Assessing the Skills Program

At the beginning of the third year, some of the children in the four- to five-year-old group turned six and joined the older group. With these additions, that group's age span was now six to nine. Also, a young assistant teacher joined our group.

Four Years at the Fifteenth Street School

In the reading and math classes, we continued with the same structure and methods that we established in the second year and monitored and assessed each student's progress. As the third year drew on, students were reading at a variety of levels. Of the approximately twenty students in the six to nine group, we realized that a few, like James mentioned earlier, had trouble with the basics of reading. We discussed these problems with their parents. When they had them tested, and they were termed "dyslexic," the parents sought private tutors to work with them.

Not all children can be expected to learn at the same rate, and there are examples of children learning to read at eight, nine or later, often when they grasp a connection between a topic of interest and the need for reading about it. In Finland and other European countries, children attend free day care until they enter school at the age of seven.

At our school, some were reading above grade level, some below. Several six- and seven-year-olds who did not attend class were hardly able to read, though we tried to work with them individually. Some children taught themselves to read without attending class. One of these was Allan, who surprised his mother. She had been concerned about his reading progress – or lack thereof.

One day, as they walked in the street, Allan burst out laughing.

"What's funny?" his mother asked.

"It's the writing on the truck: Save water. Shower with your mate."

From the books and comics that Allan spent much time with, he had decoded the key to reading on his own.

The children also learned from each other, and some imagined that they were teaching the guinea pigs to read from the *Sullivan Readers*. As the year drew to an end, we wondered how to deal with our concerns about the children who did not attend classes and did not seem to be learning to read.

By the fourth year, about twelve children from the four-to-five group had turned six, and, with two new teachers, formed a group on the fourth floor. The school now consisted of approximately fifty children: the four-to-fives on the second floor, the seven-to-nines on the third floor (with Wilbur and me as teachers), and the six-year-olds on the fourth floor. We organized the groups so that the children who knew each other could stay together.

In our classroom, Wilbur and I continued with the same structure. Overall, it was working well, despite our concerns about a few children. We evaluated the children's skills progress by monitoring each individual's work, through observation and record keeping. Tests and their attendant anxiety were not necessary. It appeared that the children in our group had developed important social and cognitive skills, as well as their abilities to conceptualize and implement complex constructs. They were able to work both cooperatively and independently. Each child developed at his/her own pace, and not everyone felt the same level of involvement.

Emerging Concerns

We held periodic parent/teacher conferences and others on request and learned of the anxiety many parents experienced about their children's reading skills. Some parents began to pressure their children to attend classes, and we began to feel pressured to have the children perform at grade level. In retrospect, it is hard to pinpoint the exact nature of this unease, how many felt this way, or what was said, but this concern raised issues about the pedagogy and philosophy of the school and the process for implementing them.

Wilbur reviewed the concepts that guided our thinking:

◄ By allowing children to move freely and select their activities according to their interests and needs, to choose when and where to do what, as long as they don't impinge on others, we eliminate at the outset the major sources of childhood resistance and rancor. If the children's experience in school is that of trust – trust built on respect – including that of the adults who attend to their needs and interests, and if the children are relatively undamaged by overly stern discipline, it will follow that they will not feel rebellious and engage in destructive behavior.

Four Years at the Fifteenth Street School

Teachers and principals can then work on maintaining and adjusting the environment, rather than focusing on controls and limitations they sometimes believe children need and like. And while children in repressive environments will indulge themselves occasionally in Dionysian frenzies of resentment, children generally prefer order to chaos.

In the children's words, the issue of control and discipline was expressed in terms of "being bossed around," and most concerns were resolved peacefully. At our school, the enthusiasm and good humor of the staff and kids contributed to an atmosphere that was light, fluid, and if we can believe what visitors tell us, veritably exuberant.

Interesting too, this was accompanied by no constraints on the expressions of longing, sadness, love, anger, discontent. We saw little evidence of the spite, destructive sarcasm, and trickery often encountered in school. In interviews with some of the graduates in later years, they comment on their surprise and dismay at encountering a harsher social atmosphere when they moved to other schools.

The children liked being in school and often did not want to leave at the end of the day. However, because they freely chose their activities and found them pleasurable, they did not always think of them as "real" school subjects or what adults may regard as "real" academics. Curiously, their experience at school was one in which "real" life was present daily. And love? Yes, love of learning in a self-regulating environment and the experience there with companions and teachers. ►

Wilbur was referring to the enthusiasm and affection for the school the children manifested through their actions and expressions.

Though most children truly loved attending the school, they were also aware that it differed from others. From friends and family members, they might hear that it was a place where children played all day, meaning that it was not an acceptable part of the culture in which learning and discipline are valued. We discussed these concerns and examined how, in fact, learning was taking place, how and why the school was different.

Voices of Children

Into this unconstrained atmosphere we had tried to graft appropriate methods for skills learning (reading, writing, math). When we established the reading and math classes, the concept of a class and class attendance represented a recognizable symbol of order to the children and parents. Since attendance was voluntary and not everyone did the same thing at the same time, it made some of the children and parents wonder whether they were, indeed, learning the skills one is supposed to learn in a classroom.

The pattern of class attendance continued, with some children going to class regularly and others, occasionally or not at all. As children decided each day whether to attend, the teachers had to discuss anew, with individuals, what would take place that day. Those who stayed out of class did not feel concerned or interested in learning the skills. They preferred to stay physically active and involved in their pursuits, and some may have felt afraid to fail. We found ourselves struggling with the conflicting principles of the need for our students to learn basic skills (or at least be exposed to instruction) and trusting them to determine their own paths and timing for this process. Many schools with the philosophy of non-compulsory education have foundered on these same issues: giving children options to attend class, while dealing with parents' expectations for the school to turn out children with skills close to grade level.

Forces at Work

We had hoped that with our plan, all the children would learn the skills in the open environment that characterized the school. As this was not happening, we began to think of alternatives to the skills program. Could we find methods to achieve academic performance while maintaining the structure of choice? This would require much thinking, experimentation, monitoring, and evaluation.

Orson felt that the present structure served well, and all would work itself out in time. Like Neill, he sincerely believed that the freedom to make choices would give the children the confidence to find their way in the world. With this outlook, he felt there was no need to make changes in our program.

Because of these concerns and disparate views, it was important at that moment in time of the school's history to review goals and expectations for achievement and find ways of refining our methods. We needed to examine the issues and develop structures to address them. I believe that, over time, a thorough examination of the program and search for alternatives could have yielded a creative solution, a way of clarifying the program, while maintaining the positive school atmosphere.

It took a while for these issues to become crystallized, given that problems were usually handled by informal talks. Everyone accepted that the authority to make final decisions rested with Orson. We could not agree on how to move forward; meetings were called with the parents and staff to try to resolve this difficult situation, and we met with some parents individually. After all the meetings and discussions, the majority voted to leave things as they were. It was a complex issue, and the adults were not able to find a solution.

Alas! Where was the Problem-Solving Committee?!

Wilbur and I thought hard about the state of the program, its future, and of the past three years and the ideas and energies invested in developing the enterprise of the school. Though we were eager to continue the work we had begun and carry forward the strong spirit of autonomy, creativity, and basic good will that characterized the school, we felt that the problems and disagreements were insurmountable. We had reached an impasse, and, with much regret, decided to part ways with the school. We were fortunate to be hired into the teacher education program at Bank Street College, where we remained until we retired in 1986.

Reflecting on Our Time at
The Fifteenth Street School

Looking back, it seems we could have had more discussions with the students about the connection between learning to read and attending class, and establishing goals with individual students, including how to attain them. Another option might have been to institute a contract program, whereby students would have the option to sign up to work for short periods. With their teachers, they would review and evaluate their work and decide whether to renew. Developing portfolios of students' work for discussion and planning is another idea. Had we had the benefit of hindsight, we might have done these and thought of other things, but events took a different course.

Wilbur reflected on these issues:

◄ The school, in its existing form was not a given, it was still in the process of becoming and what had been found to have some good and rewarding effects needed to be further refined, explored, and worked through on the actual site. After many meetings and discussions about pedagogy did not lead to any plans for changes, we felt that the only thing for us to do was to withdraw from the school. It was a great disappointment to us. We wanted to continue to work and learn in what seemed to be an interesting and perhaps important educational context. Rachel and I envisioned a lower school of children aged four to eight, where the basis would be set up for a more intensive, yet still self-regulative study program for the older children. ►

After we left, the school continued to function and grow in its own form for a number of years. We heard that the class attendance problem had been solved by giving the children a choice of committing to attend or to not be allowed to participate. The idea stems from Summerhill, where it applies to older children, ages 12 and up. They sign up for classes they want to attend, signaling a commitment to doing so. Each student receives a timetable with his schedule to help him keep track and is expected to attend so that everyone can be up to date.

Tuesday, all the kids got Together and made a surprise party for Wilbur and Rachel, Liz, Margaret, Betsy and Laura were in charge of the party. We ate ice cream and ~~████~~ donuts We also had two little plays, One was called Modern Robbers and the other one was "Voices". We played games.

☆ 2 4 6 8
WHO DO WE
APPRECIATE
WILBUR RACHEL

By Lynn

left & right: Reports in *The Squeaker Times.*

Voices of Children

2 4 6 8 WHO DO WE APPRCIATE? WILBUR RACHE

CONVERSE

"VOICE"

yesterday Wilbur and Rachel discovered the reason behind all the mysterious mumbling that has been going on for several days now. A going-away party was planned for them a few days before Memorial Day Week-End. The event was supplied with signs, flags, gifts and refreshments and skits and some recreation.

This is appropriate for older children, who can grasp the difference between not being forced to attend and attending with necessary restrictions. We heard that it was confusing to some of the younger children, who were told they would not be required to attend class, but that if they didn't come regularly they couldn't come back.

We heard that most of the children who attended the Fifteenth Street School went on to public and private schools, where their academic work was either at or close to grade level. They suffered from having to adapt to a hierarchical school structure, sit at desks, and take tests. They were surprised and frustrated by the more competitive atmosphere among the students, the pecking orders, and teasing between boys and girls.

It would be important to find ways of preparing the children for what awaited them that could, at least, mitigate the circumstances. Some of the graduates I spoke with in later years had no memory of attending class and believed they learned to read through "osmosis." They probably learned through a combination of language arts activities, reading with peers, and at home. Perhaps they do not remember that the skills sessions they attended were, indeed, classes.

Celia Converse writes about her experience at the school and beyond:

"I learned how to get along with people, to trust my own instincts, to have faith in one's own instincts, to have faith in one's own enthusiasm, which is something I had to relearn. In some way, I can't help but feel bitter because I was terribly disappointed when I left there."

Wilbur and I sometimes wondered what would have happened if we had stayed at the school and tried out different methods, and what else we might have done to improve the quality of the learning process.

Wilbur wrote:

➤ We hoped to cultivate the ability to use many resources and create new forms such as evidenced in Troll City, the Farm, Space, and the Problem-Solving Committee. These are cited as highlights as they encompassed time and many events that led to their creation. ➤

Voices of Children

These events, and others, such as the history and philosophy of the formation of the school, could have led to further inquiry into historical and theoretical connections to other topics. Studies in history and the concept of justice and the rule of law could be connected to the rules developed for the Problem-Solving Committee and the Farm of the Six. The Farm could also be a springboard for studies in ecology, agriculture, gardening, use of tools and machinery; Troll City for studies in architecture, city planning, governance; and Space for astronomy, transportation, and energy. All could be a basis for considering the past and current state of the world and the issues of the day. Some of these connections had, of course, been made at the time they occurred, and more intense reflection and research could follow as the children developed new imaginative creations. Though the children's constructs were developed in cooperation with the teachers, it can be said that their own ideas and methods were predominant.

At the same time, in the spirit of enthusiasm, we had encouraged a welter of activities to develop, and it might have been wise to curtail some of the breadth and focus more on the depth.

Wilbur commented on our work:

◄ Our quest was to attempt to find what activities children would pursue in a rational environment, which promoted the child's welfare. In truth, in doing this we spread ourselves too thin. Our day was sometimes hectic, not due to the children's exuberance, but to the sheer number of activities going on throughout the day (some requiring preparation and gathering of materials, on our part after school, along with record-keeping), and it's not impossible that superficialization of some content occurred, also a lack of focus, specificity of goals in terms of context. ►

We continued wondering about finding the best way to reconcile the concept of unequivocal freedom of choice with the responsibility for developing the skills needed to survive and succeed in society. Today, in more than 200 "democratic schools" around the world, each one has its own way of dealing with the question.

It is important for those involved in starting and running a school to be in agreement with its goals and with the methods for attaining them, as well as having a structure for communicating concerns and disagreements. Sadly, at our school, the problems that surfaced took on a magnitude and life of their own, and we could not find a suitable solution.

So many years later, Peter Gray, a research professor of psychology and author of the 2013 book *Free to Learn* read about our dilemmas and how we approached them. Reflecting on solutions that could be interesting to people thinking about Self -Directed Education today, he wrote the following:

"To me, at least, it seems that there were two mistakes made in the design and running of the school. The first mistake was to believe that Self-Directed Education (SDE) is compatible with an expectation that children learn reading and other academic material in accordance with the kind of timetable expected in coercive schools (or any timetable at all). As soon as you have that kind of expectation you have an imposed curriculum, and as soon as you have that you no longer have Self-Directed Education. There was no reason for you to know this at the time, but now we know—from the experiences of thousands of students of democratic schools and tens of thousands of un-schoolers—that everyone in SDE learns to read, but they do so on their own time course, when they find a real interest in or need for reading. There is simply no reason at all to be concerned that children aren't on a school-imposed time course for reading or anything else of an academic nature.

The other mistake, which you would have had even less reason to know was a mistake at the time, was to separate the children onto different floors by age. The key to learning in any democratic or free school is free age mixing. Young children are inspired by and learn from older ones, and vice versa. It would also have been better if you could have started with a broader age range, all mixed together. Going back to reading, the biggest inducement for reading at Sudbury Valley, for younger kids, is the presence of older kids who are reading, enjoying reading, and interacting with younger ones in ways that involve the written word."

If only Wilbur and I could have engaged Peter Gray in such discussions in 1968 or had the support of the Self-Directed Education community that exists now.

Voices of Children

Notwithstanding these events, the voices of the children at the Fifteenth Street School, expressing their enthusiasm, creativity, and social concerns, attest to the vast resources and capacities of children everywhere. I believe, as do many thoughtful educators, that our method of supporting children's self-directed efforts to learn and function strengthens their creativity and critical thought processes, as well as their social skills. In interactive environments where children and adults collaborate, their energies tap into the continually expanding potential of the human enterprise.

Bill Schenker, who attended the school for three years before moving to California, stated in an interview in 1987, that "the biggest thing was not the love of learning. Okay, that's great, but just love. That sounds stupid, trite, corny, but no, I have some strong feelings on that. I mean, I knew I didn't want to leave that place. It wasn't like I was leaving my friends or leaving my teachers – I was. But I was leaving a great place, this place where I could do my work: my work was making rockets and shooting guinea pigs to the moon or trying to figure out how I could do it. Love for learning, well, something that's far bigger and important than love for learning was a love for myself – the capacity to love myself, to feel good about myself. I felt good about myself, I felt good about other people."

Bill *(right)*, doing his "space work."

Education is represented by him (Plato),
not as the filling of a vessel,
but as the turning the eye of the soul toward the light.

– Benjamin Jowett

Chapter 8

Historical Views of Children and How They Learn

After reflecting on the Fifteenth Street School of half a century ago, we step further back in time to review the thinking that shaped the pedagogies of European and American societies. From the cultures of hunter-gatherers, to agricultural settlements, to tribes and nation states, each society aims to rear its children to fulfill its goals. The goals of European (and later American) education were to develop literate, informed citizens and to instill the young with moral principles by teaching them to follow religious precepts. As societies allocate resources according to their members' social status and often gender and race, not all segments of their populations are accorded equal access to educational opportunities. For centuries, educators and philosophers have debated conflicting views of the nature of childhood, of the thinking process, and of the merits of pedagogies for teaching the skills children need to function in their environments.

The Seventeenth Century

Going back to 1690, in his seminal writing *An Essay On Human Understanding*, the philosopher John Locke published his views on the human condition. Locke stated that, contrary to the prevailing beliefs, there were no innate ideas "stamped upon the mind" at birth. Though he likened the mind to a blank slate or tabula rasa, he believed that the mind possessed inborn faculties for processing information coming from the outside world through the senses, as well as an "internal sense" relating to inner sensations and processes. He theorized that the mind forms simple ideas and develops by combining these into more complex ones. Locke believed that by utilizing the children's own perceptions and experiences, wise teachers and parents could guide them into acquiring knowledge. Though Locke himself decried learning by lectures and memorization, educators of the time interpreted the *tabula rasa* concept to mean that the mind was a blank slate to be filled by memorizing prescribed information, ignoring the children's own curiosity and drive to learn.

The Eighteenth Century

In 1734, the German philosopher Christian von Wolff expanded on the prescriptive methodology by stating that tedious drill and repetition of basic skills were the methods that could develop the powers of the mind. Much of education has been, and still is, based on this 300-year-old concept, generally referred to as *rote learning*.

To implement this methodology, teachers had to tame the active nature of childhood and suppress children's innate energies and concerns. They adopted stern and remote demeanors to enforce obedience, and routinely inflicted corporal punishment and humiliation on their charges. All these methods are still practiced to this day.

Yet, over centuries, thinkers have taken opposite views about the nature of children and how their minds develop. In 1580, the French philosopher Michel de Montaigne stated his advice on educating boys: "Tis the custom of pedagogues to be eternally thundering in their pupil's ears, as they were pouring into a funnel, whilst the business of the pupil is only to repeat what the others have said: now I would have a tutor to correct this error, and, that at the very first, he should according to the capacity he has to deal with, put it to the test, permitting his pupil himself to taste things, and of himself to discern and choose them, sometimes opening the way to him, and sometimes leaving him to open it for himself; that is, I would not have him alone to invent and speak, but that he should also hear his pupil speak in turn. Socrates, and since him Arcesilaus, made first their scholars speak, and then they spoke to them. [Diogenes Laertius, iv. 36.]

And in 1649, the philosopher Comenius echoed Montaigne's thoughts: "The proper education of the young does not consist in stuffing their heads with a mass of words, sentences and ideas dragged together out of various authors, but in opening up their understanding to the world so that a living stream may flow from their own minds, just as leaves, flowers and fruit spring from the bud on a tree."

Whether stated or not, two basically divergent concepts of the child's mind and of the learning process have dominated the methods of education. One view holds that the mind is an empty vessel to be filled with information applied through rote methods; the other, that the developing mind grows through its own agency as it interacts with people and the environment. From the latter concept come the ideas of a child or learner-centered classroom, experiential learning, developmental interaction, self-directed learning, and democratic education.

In 1762, Jean-Jacques Rousseau, opposing the rote learning pedagogy, published his book on education: Emile. He expressed his views on human nature and society, holding that people were essentially "good," but that their character was corrupted by societal evils. Though this concept was embraced by thinkers such as Ralph Waldo Emerson and Leo Tolstoy, it still generates endless speculation and is often regarded as a naïve, romantic view of childhood and humanity in general.

Notwithstanding, Rousseau's ideas opened the door to a more optimistic view of children and their developmental circumstances, which, in turn, enabled educators to consider what conditions might foster the "good," or what we might call "growth."

Whereas, in Rousseau's time, children were generally viewed as miniature adults, Rousseau perceived that they were different creatures, maturing into adults slowly through stages of growth. He stressed the need for teachers with experience and emotional responsiveness to nurture the children's abilities in environments designed to match these stages.

Rousseau espoused the concept of individuality, noting that "every mind has its form," and believed that children should be encouraged to reason their way to their own conclusions. He wrote: "Na-

Historical Views of Children and How They Learn

ture wants children to be children before they are men...Childhood has ways of seeing, thinking and feeling, peculiar to itself, nothing could be more foolish than to substitute our ways for them."

His theories opened the door to questioning the use of repression and punishment to inculcate obedience and self-control, and to finding other methods to foster childhood development. In *Schools of Tomorrow* (1915), John Dewey wrote about Rousseau: "His insistence that education be based upon the native capacities of those to be taught, and upon the need of studying children in order to discover what these native powers are, sounded the keynote of all modern effort for educational progress. It meant that education is not something to be forced upon children and youths from without but is the growth of capacities with which human beings are endowed at birth."

Rousseau had given voice to the value of children's energies and independent thought processes, and the poet William Blake expressed his thoughts regarding the suppression that children endured in conventional schools.

The Schoolboy:
… But to go to school in a summer morn
O! It drives all joy away;
Under a cruel eye outworn,
The little ones spend the day,
In sighing and dismay
… How can the bird that is born for joy,
Sit in a cage and sing? …

The Nineteenth Century

In the intellectual climate of the early and mid-1800s, philosophers and scientists were able to study the natural world as they sought to uncover its laws and humanity's place within it. In this context, Darwin's concept of evolution, with its conclusion that humans were part of the natural order rather than a superior creation apart, caused consternation and was rejected in many quarters.

Voices of Children

Undeterred, Darwin pursued his studies of natural phenomena. He observed and noted the behavior of his newborn children and used his insights to understand and guide their development. Thus, observation of children, their nature, development, and interests led the educators Pestalozzi and Froebel to advocate that children's motor skills and intellectual abilities were integral parts of the learning process, not its obstacles. Working primarily with children aged four through six, they introduced gardening, dancing, movement, and singing, and created special tactile materials, such as blocks, puzzles, and matching, sequential self-correcting games. Requiring the active use of bodies, minds, and senses, these materials challenged and stimulated children's innate capacities in settings where they were no longer pinned down in their seats, passively receiving piecemeal information.

Then, in 1861, influenced by Rousseau, the writer Leo Tolstoy independently undertook to educate the children of the peasants (muzhiks) who worked and lived on his estate in, then, imperial Russia. Before embarking on this enterprise, he spent nine months visiting schools in Western Europe to investigate their teaching methods. He was discouraged with his findings, and when he returned to Russia, he rejected all current educational theories and developed his own methodology.

Seeking to foster a more egalitarian situation between children and adults, he established a school in which the children were free to choose whether or when to attend the school's instructional program. Tolstoy felt that much positive learning and creativity resulted from this, in spite of problems with staffing and organization.

In his biography of Tolstoy, Henri Troyat describes the school at Yasnaya Polyana: " . . . little Muzhiks appeared by twos and threes swinging their empty arms. They brought no books or notebooks with them, nothing at all, save the desire to learn. The classrooms were painted pink and blue. In one, mineral samples, butterflies, dried plants and physics apparatus lined the shelves . . . The pupils came to the classroom as though it were home, they sat where they liked, on the floor, on the window ledge, on a chair or the corner of a table, they listened or did not listen to what the teacher was saying, drew near when he said something that interested them, left the room

Historical Views of Children and How They Learn

when work or play called them elsewhere, but were silenced by their fellow pupils at the slightest sound. *Self-imposed discipline.* The lessons, if these casual chats between an adult and some children could be called that, went on from eight thirty to noon and from three to six in the afternoon and covered every conceivable subject from grammar to carpentry, by way of religious history, singing, geography, gymnastics, drawing, and composition. Once a week they all went out to the woods to study plants in the forest . . . As a disciple of Jean Jacques Rousseau, Tolstoy wanted to believe that nature was good, that all evil was a product of civilization, and that the teacher must not smother the child under the weight of learning, but must help him little by little to shape his own personality . . . Individualism, expressed in a contempt for traditional and accepted authority and an ardent love of free personal development, is at the basis of all Tolstoy's educational theories."

For his time, Tolstoy's school was totally revolutionary, taking into account the active nature of children and their interest in learning about the world by observing and exploring their environment. His own interactions showed him to be a listener and responder to the thinking and creative process of his pupils. Tolstoy accomplished all his educational work independently, and his concept and implementation seem remarkably daring, original, and forward-looking. He was a natural, inspired teacher, and his achievement set a standard for respecting children and their work.

Maria Montessori articulated the concept of the importance of children's activities with the apt phrase, "Play is the work of the child." Inspired by these pedagogies, many schools in Europe opened with similar programs.

Education in the United States

In the mid 1800s, schooling in the U.S. was primarily administered by local agencies or churches, all having diverse educational and religious agendas that influenced their efforts, educational values, and demeanors. Considering this disunity, the institution of public education, as we know it today, is relatively young, despite the fact that its roots draw on much older academic and philosophical sources. Though most schools were based on the empty vessel/rote learning theory, several were run by enlightened thinkers, who understood and supported children's developmental needs.

Notable among these is Robert Owen, who established a school for boys and girls in the New Harmony Utopian community in Indiana (1834).

Owen was influenced by the theories of the Swiss educator Pestalozzi, who based his work on the precepts first propounded by Rousseau. Pestalozzi (1805) created environments where children could express their active natures and learn through activities and objects, as well as written materials. He believed children should be free to pursue their interests and draw their own conclusions. His motto was: "Learning by head, hand and heart."

Following with similar pedagogic theories was the movement launched by Ralph Waldo Emerson's philosophy. Emerson based his ideas on his belief that people are basically good, and the goal of education is happiness. He thought the power of kindly guidance and the exertion of imagination and creativity could develop the innate powers of growth. He had faith in the ability of humans to transcend limits and reach heights of self-realization.

In 1834, Amos Bronson Alcott, a teacher in the mold of Emerson's philosophy, opened the Temple School in Boston, MA. Alcott was influenced by Pestalozzi's theories and the philosophies of Kant, Fichte, Hegel, and Locke, as well as the Quakers, with whose support he briefly ran a school. Like Emerson, Alcott believed in the development of the human spirit and the cultivation of each child's ability to reach his/her highest potential. To reach this end, he invented an instructional style of Socratic dialoguing he called "familiar and affectionate conversation." He used pictures to appeal to the imagination and asked the children to make their own.

Foreshadowing the work of Homer Lane and A.S. Neill, Alcott practiced self-government in his school by handling discipline problems through group discussions. He wrote: "Whatever children do for themselves is theirs. Originality tends to produce strength."

Historical Views of Children and How They Learn

Though Alcott gained support among Transcendentalists, his views and methods were widely criticized and rejected. In spite of his continual struggle to find employment, Alcott remained steadfast in his beliefs and their implementation.

Like-minded teachers who respected children as self-directed agents joined Owen and Alcott. Among these was Elizabeth Peabody, who founded the first public kindergarten in America (1870) based on her study of Froebel's methods and materials. Though their specific philosophies and methods differed, these nineteenth-century educators shared a respect for children's capacities and championed humane, democratic methods for educating them. The ideas of these stalwart pioneers found their way into the discourse of American educators and influenced John Dewey's thinking as he developed his theory of Progressive Education.

Impact of the Industrial Revolution

In the same period, the industrial revolution was in full swing, drawing large-scale movement of families from farms and towns to the centers of production, with a massive influx of immigrants into the same burgeoning urban centers.

Until unions and the state imposed regulations, in the late 1920s and 30s, unchecked American industry required workers, including children, to labor long hours at very low wages, in substandard working and living conditions. Children as young as eight were drafted to work in mines and factories where their health, education, and personal development suffered greatly. Mechanization and isolation deprived them of a societal context for learning even basic social skills.

Social activists and reformers became involved in improving the lives of workers and were instrumental in enacting legislation to curb inhumane working conditions. A central goal of their efforts was the institution of free, mandatory public education. Spearheading this movement was the educator and abolitionist Horace Mann, whose motives were basically humanitarian. He strongly opposed the use of corporal punishment and believed in humane methods of instruction by trained teachers. He visited many schools and came to believe in the practical benefits of a common school education by which the children of immigrants and others, deprived of opportunities, would have the chance to learn the skills and social behavior needed to attain the American dream. He believed that bringing together children of all classes and backgrounds would create opportunities for everyone to advance on an equal field. The concept of free, broad access to education was unprecedented.

After considering various pedagogical models, Mann propounded a system based on his observations of Prussian education. Schooling in Prussia was designed to prepare obedient state functionaries and generate conformist behavior. The "one size fits all" program relied primarily on rote learning. Mann and his followers saw this model as a way to introduce a uniform methodology to replace the many diverse educational methods of the time. Simultaneously, the growth of public schools would curtail the rising number of parochial schools. The Prussian school model correlated with the needs of the new industrial/factory age where skills were needed to keep the machines operating. Pupils would have to learn to be punctual, obey orders of their teachers, respond automatically to signals from bells, maintain silence, and adhere to unquestioning discipline.

Mann intended for the schools to follow a secular orientation, though teaching "Christian values" through Bible studies would be included. His ideas were opposed by clergy, who wanted a larger role for religion in the classroom, and by politicians, who feared the control of state authorities over local school systems. In spite of these objections and after a long period of debate among educators about the merits of this system, the state of Massachusetts instituted a policy of compulsory school attendance in 1850. Other states gradually followed and adopted similar models.

School Reforms

In the late 1800s, some children were attending school, while others still labored in substandard conditions. With the newly invented portable camera, the photographer/journalist Jacob Riis was able to record the hardships of children at work and the squalid conditions in which immigrants lived. His powerful photographs exposed his subjects' poverty and exploitation and fueled the movement for improving their living conditions. By the early 1900s, a strong social work movement had developed to address the cause of helping the underserved populations that filled urban centers.

Though school instruction remained modeled on the Prussian system, "child–saving" reformers helped to incorporate social supports for children, as these advocates realized that learning could not take place till some of the children's basic needs were met. In New York City, several independent groups, including school personnel, concerned citizens, and social reformers, joined forces to form the Social Progressives. This grassroots coalition aimed to provide a variety of services to immigrant and impoverished populations through the agency of the public school system. They raised funds to establish school lunch programs, playgrounds, libraries, and after-school and summer activities, as well as instruction in arts and crafts, physical education, and management skills. They addressed the needs for health care and counseling.

Most schools accepted this assistance and, over time, incorporated many of these programs into their own budgets. Today these features are accepted as part of normal school life. In 1912, the efforts of advocates such as Lilian Wald, who pioneered the Settlement House movement, resulted in instituting the federal Children's Bureau to improve the lives of children. Over time, states passed laws to curb abuses of working children, and in 1938, the Fair Labor Standards Act set a national agenda for regulating child labor.

Twentieth-Century Progressive Education

In 1897, John Dewey published his book *My Creed in Pedagogy*, in which he articulated the concept of *experiential learning*. He based his ideas on the understanding of the psychological and social make-up of the lives of children.

He states: "The child's own instincts and powers furnish the material and give a starting point for all education. Save as the efforts of the educator connect with some activity, which the child is carrying on his own initiative, independent of the educator, education becomes reduced to pressure from without. It may indeed give certain external results but cannot be called educative. Without insight into the psychological structure and activities of the individual, the educative process will, therefore, be haphazard and arbitrary."

Dewey's work brought together many of the ideas of Locke and other philosophers and educators from the hundreds of years prior, spawning the Progressive Education movement, which brought a new perspective to the lives of children and teachers. Dewey's followers explored entirely new ways of conducting a classroom, inspired by what is often referred to as "child-centered or learner-centered" pedagogy.

Following these precepts, students no longer sat at screwed-down desks in rows facing the blackboard, being lectured to. They moved about as they worked on themes that opened a variety of experiences for learning. Social Studies topics such as the neighborhood, the city, community services, ancient cultures, and the natural world formed the base for study. Textbooks followed the desks out of the classroom. Relevant books, newspapers, and reports replaced them, and child-sized tables and chairs substituted for the old desks.

The teacher's role shifted from a top-down manager of a tightly structured unit to that of an organizer of emerging ideas and activities and mentor to children, all coalescing around a common purpose. John Dewey's motto "learn by doing" was the operative phrase. (See chapter on Social Studies.)

Dewey believed that living and learning in a democratic school structure was the best preparation for participating in a democratic society. His ideas of learner-centered and interdisciplinary education were put into practice in some of the first progressive classrooms in the Laboratory School at the University of Chicago, which opened in 1896. He saw education's task as "supplying the conditions that foster growth."

The work of Freud and new studies in psychology, with information about children's stages of development and language acquisition, provided further recognition of progressive methods. These studies led educators to recognize that emotional components, such as trust, affection, motivation, pleasure, as well as anger, were important to the learning process and helped teachers and students to develop constructive forms of dealing with behavior. In 1924, Max Wertheimer published his ideas about Gestalt Theory, stating that learning takes place through insight and grasping of whole concepts.

The end of the nineteenth and beginning of the twentieth centuries saw the emergence of new ideas in science and art as well as changes and upheavals in the way societies were organized. Einstein's theory of relativity brought new concepts about the nature of the universe. The advent of electrical power altered the structures of production and travel, while transmission by wireless telegraph, radio, and telephone made possible the dissemination of information from distant parts of the world at greater speed.

In the arts, Cezanne, van Gogh, Renoir, and many others turned to observing nature and human activity for inspiration. By using recently invented metal paint tubes, artists were able to paint subjects outside of their studios, while in schools, students and teachers left the confines of the classroom to learn from people and experiences they encountered in the world outside. The artists used lively brushstrokes in their work to reflect a vision of a dynamic universe, and the active classroom reflected a vision of democracy in action. The idea of participating in movements and events in the world versus living in a fixed environment was a motivating force of the time. It was a time of seeking, of discarding old forms to uncover essential truths, of affirming the value of human life and endeavor, and also a time of discord and radical change, which broke into the violence of the Russian Revolution and World War I.

In his book *The School and Society*, Dewey reflects on the state of the world and education: "One can hardly believe there has been a revolution in all history, so rapid, so extensive, so complete . . . that this revolution should not affect education in other than formal and superficial fashion is inconceivable."

Dewey's approach to children and their education attracted a number of progressive thinkers and educators who set about developing schools to reflect those views. In 1914, Caroline Pratt established a small nursery school in New York's Greenwich Village for the purpose of studying children and developing programs suited to their needs. In 1916, she joined with Lucy Sprague Mitchell, a college dean and social activist, to found the Bureau of Educational Experiments, where teachers could learn to practice the progressive pedagogy. Located at 69 Bank Street in Manhattan, it eventually became the Bank Street College of Education. Over time, Caroline Pratt's Play School grew to accommodate children up to twelve years of age. Renamed the City and Country School, it exists to this day and continues in the tradition first laid out by Caroline Pratt.

In her book *I Learn from Children* (1948), Pratt wrote of those heady days of exploration and discovery of a new vision of education: " . . . this did not look or sound like any schoolroom. But it was very much like something else. It was a segment of grown-up activity, an office, a small factory, or perhaps office and factory combined . . . This classroom was a place where work was done. The workers could not be fastened down; they had to come and go about their various jobs, fetch supplies, seek advice, examine, compare, discuss. The work got done, not in proportion to the silence in the room, but in proportion to the responsibility of each worker to his job and to the group, some were more able, more responsible workers than others as among adults. And as among adults, there was a supervisor (not a boss, however) directing, counseling, channeling the abundant energies of these young workers, keeping the balance among personalities, keeping the schedule of the day's program and its constantly varying tasks, checking the activity of both group and individual . . . by contrast to the nailed down dependability of her (public school teacher) own classroom, here was nothing fixed, nothing stayed put, not even the furniture; above all, not the children . . . it was the traditional pattern, rather than this one, which was strange, and unfamiliar. This one was the normal pattern of human activity, adult or child."

The Little Red Schoolhouse, another progressive school, founded in 1921 by Elizabeth Irwin (with the help of John Dewey and Eleanor Roosevelt), continues to function to this day in New York City. Both Lucy Sprague Mitchell and Elizabeth Irwin were active in the creation of programs to disseminate the progressive agenda in public education. Sadly, in the 1940s, the Board of Education discontinued the Lucy Sprague Mitchell Public School Pedagogy Program. The hope that progressive education would significantly affect public education did not materialize.

Over time, the Bank Street staff refined and synthesized many of the ideas and knowledge about children and how they learn into a theory called "Developmental Interaction." It affirms the agency of the child as an independent learner with thoughts and emotions capable of creating meaning. It focuses on understanding of the maturation process and the need for teachers and settings to create democratic communities for students to explore and share the process of living and learning.

Neill, like Tostoy, believed in the rights of children to exert their agency and direct their lives and learning. Like Emerson, he believed the goal of education was happiness. Descriptions of his work are in Chapter 1.

The Twenty-First Century

During the 1960s, the public school system introduced innovations to support interactive learning. By 2000, these methods came under widespread criticism, notably by the educational researcher Diane Ravitch in her book *Left Behind: A Century of Failed School Reform* (2000). Once again, the public sector rejected and eliminated progressive education.

Ravitch worked as assistant secretary of education in the George Bush administration and participated in drafting and implementing the federal law No Child Left Behind, passed in 2001.This program, designed to close the gap between achievement levels of various social and economic groups by establishing standards of accountability, inadvertently opened the door to privatizing the public education system. It set in motion methodologies for teaching and assessment relying on stringent and frequent testing. As test results became the sole markers for judging student, teacher, and school performance, many schools geared their curriculum to teaching to the test, eschewing the arts and teachers' initiatives for cultivating children's independent, critical thought processes. Promising better test results, this movement, abetted by private sector financial support, vouchers, and charter schools, weakened the public school system's structural base and set the stage for more initiatives for privatization.

In 2009, Diane Ravitch attended a conference to evaluate results of the No Child Left Behind methodologies and heard reports of the program's widespread failures. Ravitch realized that the imposition of private for-profit efforts posed a danger to public education and was apprehensive about the possible destruction of this democratic institution established by citizens in their own communities.

In 2009, the Obama administration, aiming to improve school performance and foster innovation, passed new legislation entitled Race to the Top. Education was now conceived as a sort of marathon in which states would compete for funding by conforming to standards, such as determining teachers' status through value-added testing, lifting restrictions on the number of charter schools allowed, using the Common Core program, and closing low-achieving schools. This led to further private initiatives and the growth of a vast industry producing textbooks and testing materials. In spite of the efforts of various schools to introduce learner-centered activities, all public schools became subjected to high-stakes testing.

In her book *Reign of Error*, Ravitch describes the forces behind the privatization movement and the impact on the quality of learning it has engendered. She writes about Vivek Wahdwa, an Indian/American technology entrepreneur and academic, and his observation contrasting education in America with China. He writes that the Chinese system relies on memorization to achieve test-driven results, while in America "They learn to experiment, challenge norms,

Historical Views of Children and How They Learn

and take risks. They can think for themselves and they can innovate. This is why America remains the world leader in innovation." Ravitch responds with "The attitudes and skills that Wahdwa admires are the very ones that are sacrificed by the intensive focus on standardized testing that has been foisted on American schools by NCLB and Race to the Top."

Most followers of these programs accept the view of the learner as empty vessel, though protests by parents and some educators have led to the introduction of play and creative activities in some schools. In the private education sector, schools continue to explore various methodologies.

Rights of the Child

While many of America's children labor in their classrooms, more than two hundred million children worldwide, without legal protection, are pressed into laboring at jobs, such as brick making, garbage picking, and weaving. Often working in hazardous conditions, they are deprived of resources for development and indeed of their childhoods. To address the plight of children, the 1989 United Nations Convention on the Rights of the Child has tried to offer protection by affirming basic rights for children, including the right of freedom of thought and expression. In 2000, one hundred sixty countries approved the UN's International Labor Organization's resolution to end the worse abuses of child labor.

Yet, as these abuses continue, it is heartening that educators and other child advocates in all parts of the world are sponsoring programs, such as Computer in the Wall in India, Let Girls Learn Worldwide, and the Cambodia Bike Project, to assist children in exerting their rights to grow and develop. And forward-looking educators everywhere continue exploring ideas and methods to help empower children in their quest.

*In the following essay, the educator Alexander Khost writes about
the rights of children and self-directed education.*

"It Is Not Idealism If It Is Lived"

My involvement in self-directed education began when, in my junior year of high school, my father handed me a copy of Alexander Sutherland Neill's famous book *Summerhill, A Radical Approach to Child Rearing*. The first time I set foot in a self-directed education setting was in 2003 at the newly formed Brooklyn Free School. It was also the first time such a school had opened in New York City since the closing of the Fifteenth Street School some 25 years earlier. During the time I volunteered at the Brooklyn Free School, the staff engaged in a lot of proud talk about it being the only self-directed education school in New York City (and then in Brooklyn, when the Manhattan Free School opened). There were always these rumors and brief mentions of the Fifteenth Street School, but no one seemed to know much more about it than the fact that it existed at one point in time and had closed in the late 1970s.

When I met Rachel Rippy three years ago, I was fascinated to hear her story of the founding and operation of the Fifteenth Street School. I am pleased to be able to follow up with my research and observations about the history and present practice of self-directed education as well as its prospects for the future.

The Fifteenth Street School was part of the Free School Movement of the 1960s when Summerhill-inspired schools began cropping up throughout the United States and internationally. The spark Neill had begun with his writing spread through the movement with educators who were also important writers, such as Paul Goodman, Herbert Kohl, and Jonathan Kozol.

Many of the schools were "articulating a profound opposition to the methods and results of the public schools ... [emphasizing the] strongest possible claim for the individual child's freedom from coercive approaches to learning and social development, as expressed by the organization and techniques of most public schools." (Graubard, 1972).

Historical Views of Children and How They Learn

An example of the free school philosophy, the Fifteenth Street School functioned till the late 1970s when the movement peaked and ultimately declined.

Most notable among the schools opened during this period that were directly influenced by Summerhill were the Sudbury Valley School in 1968 in Framingham, Massachusetts, on an estate donated to the school, and the Albany Free School, in the New York State capital, in 1969.

Sudbury Valley School changed the nuances of the Summerhillian self-directed model, opting for a student-run Judicial Committee that meets to resolve conflicts and has the power to hire and fire staff. Unlike some of the American Free Schools, it discourages parent involvement inside the school grounds. Also of note, unlike Summerhill and the Free Schools, which typically have a more conventional set-up with regard to teachers, subject roles, and curricula, which children can choose to attend, the Sudbury model forbids adults from offering classes or activities, requiring all offerings to come from the suggestion of the young people in the school community. More than 80 percent of Sudbury graduates attend college.

The Albany Free School focuses on low-income inner-city children, including a large minority population. In a similar fashion to Summerhill, the school uses democratic principles through a weekly meeting and a peer-run culture committee for conflict resolution. Not only did both schools persist through the Free School Movement's decline in the late 1970s and remain open until this day, but more important, inspired the next generation of school models developed in the late twentieth century to the present day.

As the Free School Movement began its decline in the early 1970s, a new model of self-directed education was emerging. John Holt conceptualized the unschooling movement and defined the term as "taking children out of school" in an article he published in a newsletter entitled *Growing Without Schooling* (1977).

Up until this time and for some time afterward, most home-schooling parents pulled their children from the secular public schools so as to give them a religious education and tended to follow a conventional schooling model for teaching at home. However, children in unschooling settings are self-directed and choose their own experiences from which to gain an education.

As of 2014, approximately 1,800,000 children are home-schooled[1] and approximately 6,000 of these follow the unschooling model. Home education in general is on the rise.[2]

The Alternative Education Resource Organization (AERO) has been running for the past 26 years and is maintained by its founder, Jerry Mintz, who wrote: "There is no monolithic definition of democratic education or democratic schools." AERO lists about 250 democratic schools worldwide,[3] with approximately 60 Sudbury model schools.

A wide variety of self-directed models have developed, many growing out of inspiration from prior movements. For example, the anarchistic Free Skool movement "is a horizontally organized and monetarily-free network of learners" that is openly politicized and could be tied back to the anarchistic Modern School movement. It lists its influences as "classical anarchism, the new left radicalism of the 1960s, and the DIY punk ethos of 1980s radical social movements."

Other schools are influenced by back-to-the-land movements that draw on radical forms of ecology, and by popular education movements that aim for liberation of the oppressed, as well as unschoolers who seek to end the school as an institution.[4]

Agile Learning Centers (ALCs) use a new successful model of self-directed education in a school setting. The first ALC opened in 2012 in New York City. The new model was primarily inspired by the Free School Movement of the 1960s and 70s but had intentionally reinvented itself for the twenty-first century and drew inspiration from other sources, including the unschooling movement and the "Open Classroom" program that originated in British public schools. The name and model also incorporate ideas drawn from the software development process of the same name that was popularized by startup technology companies in recent years.[5]

The day starts with a school meeting. Teachers encourage students to state their intentions for the day and record them on a kanban board, a visual workflow tool. School ends with children checking the board to reflect on their intentions and record the daily activities of each member of the community in a non-binding, non-judgmental digital transcript.

Other communal agreements include blogging at the end of the week as an additional reflection tool as well as using culture committee meetings as a way to resolve conflicts, somewhat in a similar manner to free school's council meetings. With a bit less of a broadcast emphasis on politics and more on a cultural shift, the ALCs also have some resemblance to the anarchistic Modern School movement in their daily structure, and their offerings look more like those of Sudbury Valley's bottom-up, student-selected activities than the Summerhill teacher-directed optional program, adopted by the Free School Movement. There are now seven ALCs worldwide and approximately thirty startup schools based on its concepts.[6]

Agile Co-Founder Tomis Parker went on to cofound the Alliance for Self-Directed Education with some of the most influential self-directed education leaders of the time, including: Peter Gray, whose book *Free to Learn* has had a similar effect on drawing in followers as the book *Summerhill* had in 1960; Pat Farenga, who worked closely with John Holt; the writer and unschooling advocate Akilah Richards; filmmaker and writer Cevin Soling, who directed *The War on Kids* and authored *The Student Resistance Handbook*.

The organization itself looks to view this movement as more than just an educational movement but also a children's rights civil justice movement and has the goal of normalizing self-directed education and bridging the differences between the various sub-movements. Though the number of schools fitting these models is steadily growing the self-directed education model is still not even close to covering one percent of all school-aged children and very much remains a counterculture movement in the U.S. and the world.[7]

Also worthy of note are various organizations, publications, schools, and centers. In the last five or ten years there has been a rise in a movement of micro-schools, described as the "reinvention of the one-room school house."[8]

This model is somewhat like the Free School Movement of the generation before, but not necessarily committed to self-directed education per se, but rather alternatives to conventional schooling.

The International Democratic Education Network, started in 1993, holds an annual conference (IDEN) as a coming together of international schools and individuals committed to the advancement of democratic principles in education, as well as its subsidiaries, such as the European Democratic Education Community (EUDEC) and the Asia-Pacific Democratic Education Community (APDEC).[9]

The *Journal of Unschooling and Alternative Learning* (JUAL), a free, academic peer-reviewed journal that regularly publishes papers on unschooling and democratic education; and lastly the junk or adventure playgrounds, which are focused more around play than education but hold the same philosophical trust in children to direct themselves in their choices about time and interactions with others.

My own experiences as educator and parent, such as supporting my own children's desire to choose their educational setting and how to spend their time, along with my previous background as the founder of a free school, and my recent discovery of methods for children to have self-directed time outside of an educational setting in a junk playground, have helped me develop a broader picture of the import of this movement.

It is not about schooling, it is about children's rights as the next civil rights movement. It is about freeing children from the oppression of compulsory schooling as well as fear-based and permissive parenting. It is about children being able to have rightful control over their own bodies, their possessions, and respect for how they choose to spend their own time.

As a whole, the movement of self-directed education stands as a politically charged civil rights movement in the face of conventional child rearing and schooling.

The wealth of history of educated free thinkers who have researched and supported this cause is proof that this is not just a philosophy but more important, a lifestyle that has witnessed success over a two-hundred-year period.

While it sounds idealistic to profess such sentiments, this model has been proven by real people and real lives, and so it is no longer idealistic. It is simply ideal.

Historical Views of Children and How They Learn

Sources

1 http:// healthresearchfunding.org/20- incredible-unschooling- statistics/

2 http://education.oxfordre.com/view/10.1093/acrefore/9780190264093.001.0001/acrefore-9780190264093-e-80

3 http://www.educationrevolution.org/store/findaschool/democraticschools/

4 (https://freeskoolsproject.wikispaces.com/theory?response Token=8f9f1b947ec44b73e6089c01648850b5)

5 https://en.wikipedia.org/wiki/Agile_software_development

6 http:// agilelearningcenters.org/#map

7 https://www.self-directed.org/,

8 http://educationnext.org/school-disruption-on-small-scale-micro-schools-nuvu-wildflower/.

9 http://www.idenetwork.org/

Looking to the Future

Today, as the twenty-first century unfurls, we stand on the edge of the unknown world of future technology and political action. Facing these changes, children will need sharpened skills for thinking and imagining, and the freedom to direct their lives in a social context. Our hopes lie in following the courageous thinkers who, throughout history, have advocated for the rights of children to speak and have their voices be heard.

United Nations Rights of the Child

Article 12: Parties shall assure to the child who is capable of forming his or her views the right to express those views freely in all matters affecting the child, the views of the child being given due weight in accordance with the age and maturity of the child.

Article 13: The child shall have the right to freedom of expression; this right shall include freedom to seek, receive and impart information and ideas of all kinds, regardless of frontiers, either orally, in writing or in print, in the form of art, or through any other media of the child's choice. This right may be subject to certain regulations related to the rights and reputations of others.

Article 14-1: Parties shall respect the rights of the child to freedom of thought, conscience and religion.

Article 14-2: Parties shall respect the rights and duties of the parents and, when applicable, legal guardians, to provide direction to the child in the exercise of his or her right in a manner consistent with the evolving capacity of the child.

Closing Thoughts

For want of ability to express it in full, I have left out a great deal of the day-to-day flavor of life at our school. I cannot do justice to the vitality, sounds, and sheer energy, the ups and downs of moods and behavior, and the wide spectrum of feelings and perceptions experienced by children and teachers.

Wilbur concludes:

◄ I regard the record of the children at the Fifteenth Street School, working, playing, interacting for long periods of time without adult supervision, as the most salient demonstration of their capacity to regulate their own behavior.

The children's demeanor is impossible to convey by words.

The expressions of joy, exuberance and intensity in their faces and body language are palpable in photographs that reveal the children's vibrant engagement with the multidimensional world of relationships and things, with the materials to be formed, transformed. ►

Historical Views of Children and How They Learn

References

Applebee, Arthur N., ed. 1978. Fantasy and distancing. The child's concept of story: Ages two to seventeen. Chicago, IL: Chicago University Press.

Bernstein, Leonard. 1988. Humphrey Burton interview, Facebook.

Bronowski, Jacob. 1956. The creative mind. Science and human values. New York: Harper and Row.

Burton, Judith. 2005. The integrity of personal, experience, or the presence of life in art. http://ed.arte.gov.tw/uploadfile/Periodical/1131_%E7%AC%AC%E4%B8%89%E5%8D%B7%E7%AC%AC%E4%BA%8C%E6%9C%9F9-36.pdf.

Casper, Virginia & Theilheimer, Rachel. 2010. Early childhood education: learning together. New York: McGraw-Hill.

Comenius, John Amos. 2912. The Great didactic. London: Forgotten Books (Classic Reprint).

De Montaigne, Michel. 2015. The education of children. London: Forgotten Books.

Dewey, John. 1897. My pedagogic Creed. School Journal. 54, pp. 77-80.

Dewey, John. 1899/1980. The school and society. Carbondale, IL: Southern Illinois University Press.

Flesch, Rudolf. 1955/1986. Why Johnny can't read. New York: HarperCollins.

Froebelweb.org. http://www.froebelweb.org/web2000.html. Accessed October 13, 2017.

Gardner, Howard. 2006. Frames of mind: The theory of multiple intelligences. New York: Basic Books.

Gopnik, Alison. July 30, 2016. What babies know about physics and foreign languages. New York Times, Sunday Review. https://www.nytimes.com/2016/07/31/opinion/sunday/what-babies-know-about-physics-and-foreign-languages.html.

Gopnick, Alison & Meltzoff, Andrew. 1997. Words, thoughts, and theories. Cambridge, MA: MIT Press.

Graubard, Allen. September 1972. The free school movement. Harvard Educational Review. Vol. 42, Issue 3, pp. 352-353.

Gray, Peter. 2013. Free to learn: Why unleashing the instinct to play will make our children happier, more self-reliant, and better students for life. Philadelphia, PA: Basic Books.

Greenberg, Daniel. 1995. Free at last: The Sudbury Valley School. Framingham, MA: Sudbury Valley School Press.

Gwathmey, Edith & Mott, Ann-Marie. 2000. Visualizing experience. Revisiting a progressive pedagogy. Nancy Nager & Edna Shapiro, eds. New York: Teachers College Press, pp. 139-160.

Hawkins, David. February, 1965. Messing about in science. Science and Children 2(5).

Holt, John. 1995. How children learn. Cambridge, MA: Da Capo Press.

Holt, John. 1997. Growing without schooling: A record of a grassroots movement. Vol. 1, Aug. 1977- Dec. 1979. John Holt Associates.

Jowett, Benjamin. 1892. Plato, the dialogues of Plato, in 5 vols. London: Oxford University Press.

Kamii, Constance, with Joseph, Linda. 2004. Young children continue to reinvent arithmetic, 2nd grade. 2nd ed. New York: Teachers College Press.

Lane, Homer. 1928. Talks to parents and Teachers. London: George Allen and Unwin.

Leonard, George. 1968. Education and ecstasy. New York: Delacorte Press.

Lord, Lois. 1958/1996. Collage and construction in school: Preschool/junior high. New York: Bank Street College of Education reprint.

Lowenfeld, Viktor & Brittain, W. Lambert. 1947. Creative and mental growth. New York: MacMillan Publishing Company.

McArdle, Felicity & Wright, Susan Kay. 2014. First literacies: Art, creativity, play, constructive meaning-making. Literacy in the arts: Retheorising learning and teaching. Georgina Barton. ed. New York: Springer, pp. 21-37.

Miller, Ron. 2002. Free schools, free people: Education and democracy after the 1960's. Albany, NY: State University of New York Press.

Moulin, Daniel. 2014. Leo Tolstoy. New York: Bloomsbury Academic.

Mumford, Lewis. 1967. The myth of the machine. Vol. 1. New York: Harcourt Brace Jovanovich.

Neill, A. S. 1916. A dominie's log. New York: R. McBride & Co.

Neill, A. S. 1939. The problem teacher. London: Herbert Jenkins.

Neill, A. S. 1960. Summerhill: A radical approach to child rearing. New York: Hart Publishing Company.

Piaget, Jean & Inhelder, Bärbel. 2000. The psychology of the child. 2nd ed. New York: Basic Books.

Powell, John Wesley. 1895. The exploration of the Colorado River and its canyon. Washington, DC: Smithsonian Institution.

Pratt, Caroline. 1948. I learn from children: An adventure in progressive education. New York: Grove Paperback.

Ravitch, Diane. 2013. Reign of error: The hoax of the privatization movement and the danger to America's public schools. New York: Knopf.

Ravitch, Diane. 2000. Left behind: A century of failed school reform. New York: Simon & Schuster.

Rippy, Wilbur. 1972-73. The legacy of Paul Goodman. Change. Publisher TK.

Rippy, Wilbur. 1975. Experience and creative language. Dimensions of language. Bronx, New York: Agathon Press.

Rogoff, Barbara. 2014. Learning by observing and pitching in to family and community endeavors: An orientation. Human Development. 57: 69-81. DOI: 10.1159/000356757.

Spolin, Viola. 1963/1999. Improvisations for the theater. Chicago, IL: Northwestern University Press.

Tolstoy, Leo. 1861/1904. The complete works of Count Tolstoy. Vol. 4. Boston: D. Estes & company.

Troyat, Henri. 1967. Leo Tolstoy. New York: Doubleday and Company.

Vygotsky, Lev. 1978. Mind in society. Cambridge, MA: Harvard University Press.

Weir, Ruth Hirsch. 1970. Language in the Crib. Mouton de Gruyter.

Wilson, Edward O. 1984. Biophilia. Cambridge, MA: Harvard University Press.

References

About the Authors

In 1964, Rachel and Wilbur Rippy helped to found the Fifteenth Street School. Subsequently, they joined the graduate faculty at the Bank Street College of Education and retired in 1986. Rachel currently lives in New York City.

Made in the USA
Middletown, DE
10 December 2021

54955728R00195